Research Navigator™ Guide for

Social Gerontology
A Multidisciplinary Perspective
Seventh Edition

Nancy R. Hooyman
University of Washington

Asuman Kiyak
University of Washington

PEARSON

Boston | New York | San Francisco
Mexico City | Montreal | Toronto | London | Madrid | Munich | Paris
Hong Kong | Singapore | Tokyo | Cape Town | Sydney

For related titles and support materials, visit our online catalog at
www.ablongman.com

To obtain permission(s) to use material from this work, please submit
a written request to Allyn and Bacon, Permissions Department,
75 Arlington Street, Suite 300, Boston, MA 02116 or fax your request
to 617-848-7320.

Between the time Web site information is gathered and then published,
it is not unusual for some sites to have closed. Also, the transcription
of URLs can result in unintended typographical errors. The publisher
would appreciate notification where these errors occur so that they
may be corrected in subsequent editions.

ISBN   0-205-44363-X

Printed in the United States of America

10 9 8 7 6 5 4 3 2 1   08 07 06 05 04

Contents

Using Research Navigator   iv

CHAPTER 1	THE GROWTH OF SOCIAL GERONTOLOGY	1
CHAPTER 2	HISTORICAL AND CROSS-CULTURAL ISSUES IN AGING	9
CHAPTER 3	THE SOCIAL CONSEQUENCES OF PHYSICAL AGING	17
CHAPTER 4	MANAGING CHRONIC DISEASES AND PROMOTING WELL-BEING IN OLD AGE	23
CHAPTER 5	COGNITIVE CHANGES WITH AGING	29
CHAPTER 6	PERSONALITY AND MENTAL HEALTH	35
CHAPTER 7	LOVE, INTIMACY, AND SEXUALITY IN OLD AGE	41
CHAPTER 8	SOCIAL THEORIES OF AGING	47
CHAPTER 9	THE IMPORTANCE OF SOCIAL SUPPORTS: FAMILY, FRIENDS, NEIGHBORS, AND COMMUNITIES	53
CHAPTER 10	CAREGIVING	61
CHAPTER 11	LIVING ARRANGEMENTS AND SOCIAL INTERACTIONS	67
CHAPTER 12	PRODUCTIVE AGING: PAID AND NONPAID ROLES AND ACTIVITIES	73
CHAPTER 13	DEATH, DYING, BEREAVEMENT, AND WIDOWHOOD	81
CHAPTER 14	THE RESILIENCE OF ELDERS OF COLOR	89
CHAPTER 15	THE RESILIENCE OF OLDER WOMEN	97
CHAPTER 16	SOCIAL POLICIES TO ADDRESS SOCIAL PROBLEMS	103
CHAPTER 17	HEALTH AND LONG-TERM CARE POLICY AND PROGRAMS	109

Research Navigator™ Guide for Social Gerontology: A Multidisciplinary Perspective, Seventh Edition, is designed to integrate the content of the book with the resources of Research Navigator, a collection of research databases, contemporary publications, and instruction available to you online at www.researchnavigator.com.

What You Can Do with Research Navigator

- **Search EBSCO's ContentSelect,** a database consisting of scholarly publications (such as *The Gerontologist* and *Journal of Aging and Social Policy*) and general interest publications (such as *Newsweek,* the *Christian Science Monitor,* and the *Nation*). You can search by keyword or topic, and articles can be cut, pasted, emailed, or saved for later use.
- **Search the *New York Times*** by keyword for full-text articles that have appeared in the previous year in the *New York Times.*
- **Search the "Best of the Web" Link Library,** a collection of web links, organized by academic subject and key terms. Selected links have been reviewed for relevance and credibility, and are monitored and updated as necessary on a weekly basis.
- **Get Research Help** on all aspects of the research process, among them finding a topic, gathering sources, organizing, drafting, and citing sources.

Research Aids in the Guide

As you read the guide, you'll see several features connecting you to the Research Navigator website. Use these features to explore concepts in the text and the research being done in the field of gerontology.

- **An annotated bibliography of recommended articles.** These additional readings, from both popular and scholarly sources, let you pursue chapter topics and related material in more depth. You'll find these bibliographies, which serve as a useful starting point for research, in the Research Navigator guide.

- **Applied research exercises.** These suggestions provide more practice using the databases in Research Navigator, and move students beyond the book to library and field research.

Registering with Research Navigator

Research Navigator is simple to use and easy to navigate. The goal of Research Navigator is to help you complete research assignments or research papers quickly and efficiently. The site is organized around the following tabs:

- Home
- Research Process
- Finding Sources
- Using Your Library

In order to begin using Research Navigator, you must first register using the personal access code that appears in the front cover of this book.

You can find your personal access code to Research Navigator on the inside front cover of this guide. To register, follow these steps.

1. Go to http://www.researchnavigator.com. Click "Register" under new users on the left side of the home page screen.

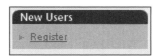

2. Enter the access code exactly as it appears on the inside front cover of your book or on your access card. (Note: Access codes can only be used once to complete one registration. If you purchased a used text, the access code may not work.)

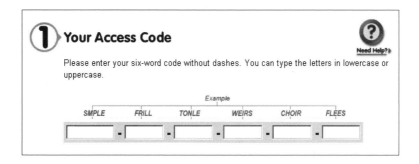

3. Follow the instructions on screen to complete your registration—you may click the Help button at any time if you are unsure how to respond.

4. Once you have successfully completed registration, write down the Login Name and Password you just created and keep it in a safe place. You will need to enter it each time you want to revisit Research Navigator.

5. You now have access to all the resources in Research Navigator for six months. Each time you enter Research Navigator, log in by simply going to the "Returning Users" section on the left side of the homepage and type in your LoginID and Password.

Getting Started

Once you have selected your research topic, you are now ready to gather information. From Research Navigator's home page, you have access to three exclusive databases of source content.

EBSCO's ContentSelect Academic Journal and Abstract Database

- Choose a subject database from the pull-down menu; then enter the key word you wish to search. Click on "Go."

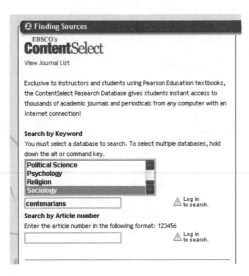

- Now you'll see a list of articles that match your search. From this page you have all of the options shown below.

- An article in ContentSelect looks like this. Scroll down to get the full text of the article.

The *New York Times*

- Choose a subject from the pull-down menu to search for a *New York Times* article by subject.

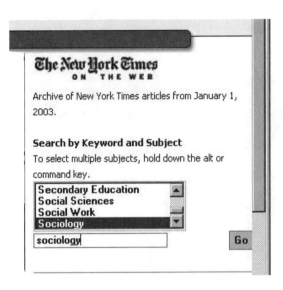

- Here is an example of the results list from the *New York Times* archives searched by subject. The articles are sorted in chronological order, with the most recent one first.

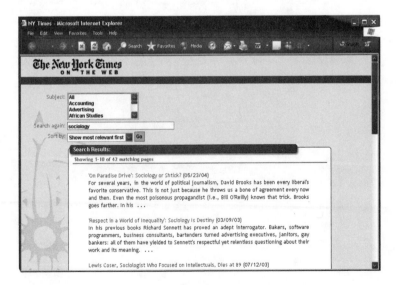

- Search for a *New York Times* article by entering a keyword.

- Here is an example of the results list for the *New York Times* search by keyword.

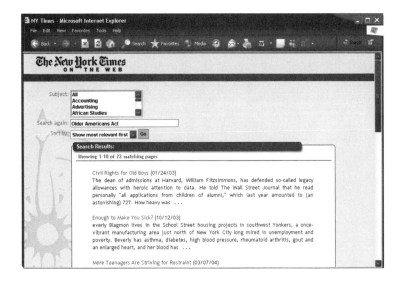

"Best of the Web" Link Library

- Use this feature to find useful websites for a particular subject.

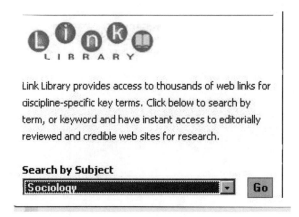

- Choose a subject from the pull-down list; then click on the first letter of your key term to locate it.

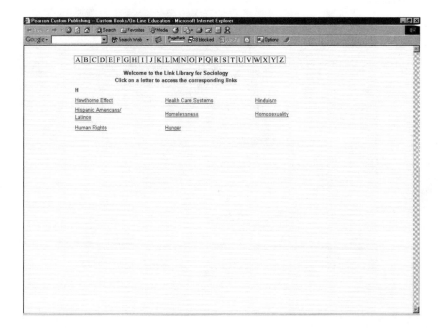

- Here is a list of annotated websites available on your topic. Click on the site you're interested in.

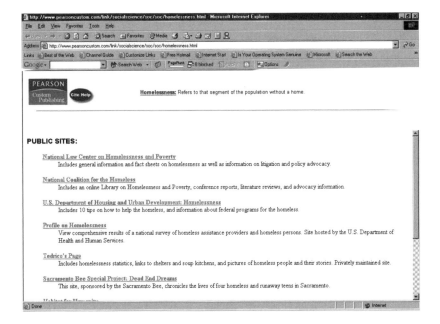

Understanding the Research Process

Get help doing research and documenting sources. Here you'll find such topics as

- Gathering Data
- Searching the Internet
- Evaluating Sources

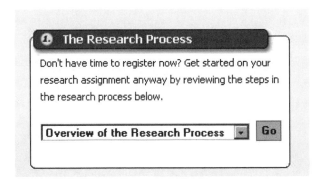

- Organizing Ideas
- Drafting the Paper
- Documenting your sources in APA, MLA, CMS and CBE formats
- Practicing Academic Integrity
- Revising
- Proofreading

NOTE: Please be aware that the Research Navigator site undergoes frequent changes as new and exciting options are added to assist with research endeavors. For the latest information on the options available to you on Research Navigator, visit www.ablongman.com/researchnavigator.

The Growth of Social Gerontology

Centenarians

Suggested Reading

Popular

1. Schneider, J. 100 and Counting. *U.S. News & World Report,* 2002, *132,* No. 19, p. 86.

The author discusses centenarians and the life expectancy of the 4.2 million oldest old in the U.S. Cite three additional articles that examine the role of lifestyle and genes in longevity and the outlook for those people age 100 and older—the fastest-growing subpopulation of the elderly. (*AN 6718523*).

2. Christensen, D. Making Sense of Centenarians. *Science News,* March, 10, 2001, *159,* No. 10, p. 156. (*AN 4196793*).

The author discusses the percentage of centenarians who live independently, who live with some limitations and who are totally dependent. Cite four other studies that examine people's lifestyles in terms of nutrition, social networks and genetics.

3. Wagner, C. The Centenarians Are Coming. *Futurist,* 1999, *33,* No. 5 (*AN 1787257*).

Jeanne Calment was born in Aries, France in 1875—before the Eiffel Tower was built. Until her death in 1997 at age 122, she had broken all human longevity records. The author examines a major study undertaken by the IPSEN Foundation of France. Find other studies that look at declining mortality rates and how this shift will have major effects on business, including the insurance, leisure and healthcare sectors.

Scholarly

1. Samuelson, S.-M.; Alfredson, B. Bauer; Hagberg, B.; Samuelsson, G.; Nordbeck, B.; Brun, A.; Gustafson, L.; Risberg, J.. The Swedish Centenarian Study: A Multidisciplinary Study of Five Consecutive Cohorts at the Age of 100. *International Journal of Aging & Human Development,* 1997, 45, No. 3, p. 223–255 (*AN 3265858*).

This study about centenarians in Sweden describes the 100+ population from physical, social and psychological points of view. It also identifies factors that predict future survival. Centenarians are characterized with various health conditions and diverse degrees of autonomy and life satisfaction. Cite three other studies that examine the health, attitude and resiliency of this age group.

2. Fredrickson, B. The value of positive emotions. *American Scientist,* 2003, *91,* No. 4 (*AN 10029857*).

Psychologist Fredrickson argues that positive emotions allowed our ancestors to broaden their minds and build resources—intellectual, physical and social—that served them in good stead during hard times. Discuss how the emerging science of positive psychology is coming to understand why it is good to feel good and how it contributes to longevity.

Applied Research Exercises

1. By 2010, there will be as many seniors as there are people under the age of 20. In the early 1900s, when current centenarians were young children, the population, in terms of age, was in the shape of a steep triangle, with the vast proportion being young and only a very few reaching very old age. Approximately 3 million of those young children are now centenarians, causing a "rectangularization" of the population—more and more people living beyond the vulnerable childhood years and achieving old age, so that the older group at the top ages nearly equals the bottom. The New England Centenarian Study, conducted by the Harvard Medical School, Division on Aging, examines this phenomenon. Cite two other studies on longevity that refer to the cognitive and personality profiles, genetic transfer and fa-

Research Navigator Guide: Social Gerontology

milial traits of centenarians. Discuss what countries and/or U.S. regions are examined in these studies.

2. In the June 28, 1999 issue of the *Christian Science* Monitor, staff writer Laurent Belsie shows how centenarians are breaking down long-held beliefs about aging. Discuss five of these myths demonstrating why they are no longer true and substantiate with concrete examples. *(AN 1971038)*

3. The American Federation for Aging Research's website, www.infoaging .org lists the following under its *Healthy Aging* heading:

Nutrition	Smoking
Exercise	Vision
Sleep	Hearing
Stress	Oral Health
Alcohol	Immunization

Choose three of the above topics and describe why each topic contributes to or detracts from the likelihood of a person reaching age 100.

International Aging

Suggested Reading

Popular

1. Fact Sheets. Challenges of Global Aging. Administration on Aging website: http://www.aoa.gov/press/fact/alpha/fact_global_aging.asp

54% of the world's older persons live in Asia; 24% live in Europe. These expanding numbers of the oldest old are unprecedented. This 21st century phenomenon can be attributed to advances in science, technology and medicine, education and nutrition. The AoA is the official federal agency dedicated to policy development, planning and the delivery of supportive home and community based services to older persons and their caregivers. Discuss two collaborative activities of the AoA with other countries and what steps are being taken to implement "The International Plan of Action on Ageing".

2. Takahashi, R. How bathing accidents occur among old people. Tokyo Metropolitan Institute of Gerontology website: http://www.tmig.or.jp

Japan is experiencing the most rapid rate of population aging in the world. The number of in-house drowning accidents among healthy elders is increasing in Japan. It is reported that 100% of people in Japan soak in the tub more than three times a week whereas only 23% of people in the United States take soaking baths. Bathing accidents among healthy elders in Japan is becoming a serious health issue. Find three articles that discuss the rise of in-house accidents among elders in other countries and what strategies are being developed to prevent these accidents.

3. Takayama, H. The Okinawa Way. *Newsweek* Jan. 24, 2003, *141,* No. 2 (*AN8822084*).

The author reports on the book *The Okinawa Program,* which found that heart disease, breast cancer, and prostate cancer were rare in Okinawa's elderly. Give five examples of why the authors suggest Americans might try to live more like the Okinawans. Also elaborate on the research findings and how this healthy lifestyle is being threatened today.

Scholarly

1. Robine, J-M.; Saito, Y. Survival Beyond Age 100: The Case of Japan. *Population & Development Review,* 2003 (Supplement) *29.* (*AN 9708473*).

The authors investigate the nature of data on human mortality, focusing on the oldest old in Japan. Find three other studies from different countries that focus on life expectancy and the reasons behind increasing life spans in most countries.

2. The U.S. Census Bureau issued a report in November 2001, "The Aging World," which is on the website http://www.census.gov/prod/2001pubs/p95–01–1.pdf. Go to page 5 and select five of the 20 questions on aging. Give not only the answers that appear on page six but also elaborate with other facts.

3. "The Aging World" also states that the world's older population is growing at a rapid pace: 77% of the world's net gain of elderly individuals from July 1999 to July 2000—615,000 people monthly—occurred in developing countries. Discuss the challenges for developing countries as their older populations increase, and the dynamics of this rapid growth on developing countries' resources.

Applied Research Exercises

1. Italy now has the largest proportion of people over age 65 among all countries, 18% in 2000. Greece, Sweden and Japan each have approximately 17% of their populations age 65 and over. The United States has less than 13%. Find three research reports that address this issue and elaborate on the findings.

2. Discuss the widening of the gender differential in life expectancy in three industrial and three developing countries. What impact will this have on future populations of older adults in these countries?

3. Search the Web for pension policies by American companies and how they have changed over the past ten years. To what extent have these changes been affected by population change vs. economic pressures? How will these changes affect future retirees?

Successful Aging

Suggested Reading

Popular

1. Kolata, G. Gains on heart disease leave more survivors, and questions. *New York Times,* Jan. 19, 2003.

The author provides dramatic evidence from NIH statistics on the reduction of deaths from heart attacks and strokes since 1970. Interviews with several experts in health epidemiology reveal that both heart attacks and strokes are becoming a disease of the oldest old, and these are no longer considered to be fatal conditions. The impact of an increase in older adults with chronic diseases is discussed in the article. With better methods of detection, doctors are picking up heart attacks and strokes that would have gone unnoticed in previous years.

2. Kantrowitz, B. Health for Life: Living Longer, Living Better. *Newsweek* Special Issue on Aging Fall/Winter2001 Special Edition, 138 No. 11, p. 4 (*AN5123430*).

This special issue examines the biology of aging and what happens to the body and brain as they get older. Explores the particular challenges of middle-aged Americans in maintaining healthy habits and stories on exercise and diet offer the latest research on what works and the best advice on how to get started. Examines how scientists are beginning to illuminate the process of aging.

3. Rowe, John W. The New Gerontology. *Science* 10/17/97, *278,* No. 5337, p. 367 (*AN 9710303535*).

A "new gerontology" is emerging that goes beyond the prior preoccupation with age-related diseases such as Alzheimer's to include a focus on senescence, the progressive nonpathological, biological and physiological changes that occur with advancing age and that influence functional status as well as the development of disease. There are significant qualitative as

Research Navigator Guide: Social Gerontology

well as quantitative differences between age-related (senescent) and disease-related (pathological) processes.

Scholarly

1. Strawbridge, W. J., Wallhagen, M. I., Cohen, Richard D. Successful Aging and Well-being: self-rated compared with Rowe and Kahn. *The Gerontologist* 2002, *42,* No. 6, p. 727–733 (*AN 8736534*).

This research evaluates the utility of two different definitions of successful aging in predicting well-being. Using data from the Alameda County study in California, the authors compare subjective definitions of well-being in old age vs. objective criteria from the successful aging paradigm. They found that absence of chronic diseases and ability to perform ADLs were key factors in successful aging for both definitions. However, many elderly subjects in this study rated themselves as aging successfully, although they would not be classified as such in the theoretical model.

2. Various "The Paradox of *'Successful Aging'*: A Critical Look at Neglected Dimensions." *The Gerontologist,* 1999, *39,* No. 1: 57–60 (*AN 2446393*).

Presents abstracts of several studies on successful aging submitted to the 52nd Annual Scientific Meeting of the Gerontological Society of America on November 19–23, 1999 in San Francisco, California: 'Images of Successful Aging,' by M. Minkler; 'Aging Successfully: Its Unintended and Negative Consequences,' by M. Holstein; "Successful Aging' and People With Disabilities: What's the Message,' by P. Faden.

3. Kahn, R. L. Guest Editorial: On Successful Aging and Well-Being: Self-Rated Compared With Rowe and Kahn. *The Gerontologist* 2002 42: No. 6, p. 725–726.

Presents conflicting definitions of successful aging and some of the errors that researchers have made in operationalizing this concept in their studies. This is a good attempt at integrating different definitions of successful aging.

Applied Research Exercises

1. What do gerontologists mean by successful aging? Given the ambiguity of the term "success" itself, it is not surprising there is no single well-accepted definition or model of successful aging. It has been defined as "adding life to the years" and "getting satisfaction from life". Others have defined it in terms of multiple physiological and psychosocial variables. Read the two following articles and compare and contrast their definitions of "successful aging."

Research Navigator Guide: Social Gerontology

    a. Rowe, J. W. & Kahn, R. L. (1997) "Successful Aging." *The Gerontologist 37,* No. 4: 433–440.

    b. Brody, J. E. (1996). Good habits outweigh genes as key to a healthy old age. *New York Times.* February 28, C, 9:1.

2. Discuss the debate in defining "successful aging" in terms of productive activities vs. spiritual and existential activities (i.e. these may not always be "productive" but often provide the individual a great deal of satisfaction, such as prayer, meditation, a walk in the woods). Cite three studies since 1996 that support productive aging as activities that contribute to society (both paid and nonpaid). Cite three studies since 1996 that show the importance of personally satisfying activities as part of successful aging.

3. Social gerontology has three primary, complementary tasks: to understand: (1) the aging process as an individual experience; (2) the social, political, and economic positions of older people; and (3) the social consequences that result from an aging population. Cite three specific studies that encompass each of these tasks related to understanding the individual, structural and social consequences of aging. What does each of these studies conclude about the aging process?

Research Navigator Guide: Social Gerontology

Historical and Cross-Cultural Issues in Aging

Old Age in Asian Countries

Suggested Reading

Popular

1. Fang, B. The parent sitters club. *U.S. News & World Report,* 09/04/2000, *129,* No. 9, p. 28 (*AN 3483860*).

As the older population grows in China, more services are evolving to care for aging parents while adult children work. One such business, the "Nice Nanny Service", pairs college students with older people. Give examples of some social customs in China that influence the way older people are regarded, according to this article. How might these customs create tension among families who use the "Nice Nanny Service"?

2. Kary, T. Total eclipse of the son. *Psychology Today,* Feb 2003, *36,* No. 1, p. 20 (*AN 8735922*).

Divergent trends in modern Japan have influenced intergenerational communication in this country with a large proportion of people aged 65 and older. This article discusses the cultural gap between younger and older people in Japan. What views do young Japanese people express about their parents? What is the "Hikikomori Syndrome"?

3. Takayama, H. The Okinawa way. *Newsweek,* 1/13/2003, *141,* No. 2, p. 54 (*AN 8822084*).

In a country with one of the largest proportions of centenarians, the city of Okinawa has the highest proportion of all. The Japanese author of this article discusses healthy lifestyle factors in Okinawa that give it this distinction. What concerns does the author express regarding health trends in Okinawa as its people adopt more elements of the American lifestyle? What efforts are being made to preserve their traditional lifestyle?

Scholarly

1. Chee, Y. Elder care in Korea: the future is now. *Ageing International,* Summer/Fall 2000, *26,* No. 1/2, p. 25 (*AN 5367407*).

The influence of Korea's cultural heritage on aging in this country is examined. The author discusses the development of services aimed at older people. What argument does the author make regarding balancing public policy and family care for older people? What support is offered for this argument, and what does it tell us about the culture of aging in Korea?

2. Hui, Y. The case in Hong Kong. *Ageing International,* Spring 2000, *25,* No. 4, p. 47 (*AN 4773896*).

The focus of this article is on trends in aging in Hong Kong, including the growth of policies and services aimed specifically at caring for its older citizens. What demographic profiles of older people are highlighted in this article? What services are available to older people in Hong Kong?

3. Leokoff, S. Graying of Japan: Choju Shakai. *Ageing International,* Summer/Fall 2000, *26,* No. 1/2, p. 10 (*AN 5367393*).

The author addresses the changing nature of intergenerational relations in Japan. What are some motivations of adult parents in caring for older parents in Japan? What kinds of government-subsidized non-profit facilities are available for its growing population of older people?

Applied Research Exercises

1. Based on the articles described above, make a list of traditional cultural values and customs in Japan, China, and Korea that are different from Western values and customs. For each of these values and customs, discuss what conflicts may arise if older adults in these countries maintain these traditional values and customs, but younger generations adopt Western customs and values.

Research Navigator Guide: Social Gerontology

2. Search the Internet for the latest population statistics about Japan, China, and Korea (e.g. U.N., national census data), comparing these to U.S. Census Bureau statistics (based on the 2000 Census) for the age and gender distribution of each country's population. Compare the proportion of people across these four countries within each gender for the following age groups: children, young adults, middle-aged, old-old, oldest-old (or approximately 18 and under, 20–45, 45–65, 65–85, 85 and older). What differences emerge when you compare these countries? How might these differences influence the availability of a workforce and the need for services for their older citizens?

Grandparenting in Different Cultures

Suggested Reading

Popular

1. Iyer, P. Grandmothers. *American Scholar,* Autumn 2003, *72,* No. 4, p. 93 (*AN 11077128*).

The role of grandparents in Japan is discussed, focusing on the relationship between grandmothers and grandchildren. What insights does the author give into younger people's attitudes toward grandparents in Japan? How do these attitudes affect grandparents' involvement in the lives of their grandchildren?

2. Miller, S. In Spain, grandparents begin leaving home. *Christian Science Monitor,* 3/11/2002, *94,* No. 73, p. 7 (*AN 6305587*).

This article discusses a changing trend in Spain, where more grandparents are living in nursing homes instead of moving into the homes of their children and grandchildren. What social and demographic factors contribute to this change? Describe how this change in living arrangements might also change the role of grandparents in Spain.

3. York, S. Latino grandparents in picture books by Latino writers. *Library Media Connection,* Apr/May 2003, *21,* No. 7, p. 40 (*AN 9467571*).

This article presents books by Latino writers that discuss the importance of grandparents in their culture. Select one of the featured writers and discuss how his/her discussion of the role of grandparents highlights the culture of grandparenting in Latino communities.

Scholarly

1. Strom, R., Shirley, K. Intergenerational learning and family harmony. *Educational Gerontology,* Apr/May 2000, *26,* No. 3, p. 261 (*AN 3323532*).

Differences in perceptions about grandparents across cultures are examined by comparing families in China and the United States. What differences are highlighted by this article? How can the findings of this study be used to plan educational programs for older people?

2. Peterson, C. Grandfathers' and grandmothers' satisfaction with the grandparenting role: Seeking new answers. *International Journal of Aging & Human Development,* 1999, *49,* No. 1, p. 61 (*AN 2632746*).

The author examines Australian elders' satisfaction in their roles as grandparents. What factors were found to affect attitudes toward grandparenting, and did these differ between men and women? How might these attitudes toward grandparenting differ from those in the United States?

3. Giaquinto, E., Ryan, E., K. Gesen et al. The culturally constructed experience of old age: Italy and the U.S. *The Gerontologist,* Oct 99, *39,* No. 5, p. 201 (*AN 2446480*).

A group of abstracts from a meeting of the Gerontological Society of America are presented, focusing on differences between elders in Italy and the United States. List some cultural activities that are described in the article; to what extent do national differences reflect variations in the aging process in these countries? Discuss the way the article characterizes old age as a cultural construction.

Applied Research Exercises

1. Interview at least five young adults (ages 18–30) who had regular contact while growing up with U.S.-born grandparents whose native language was English, and five whose grandparents were immigrants or ethnic minorities who did not speak English as a first language. In an attempt to determine the impact that grandparents' cultural background plays on their grandchildren, ask the following questions:
   a. What was the ethnic/national background of your grandparents?
   b. If not English, what was their native language, and did they speak this language in your presence?
   c. Did you learn to speak that language?
   d. On average, how much time did you spend with this/these grandparent(s) while growing up?
   e. What cultural values did you adopt from your grandparents?
   f. If your grandparents need help in their old age (or if they did when they were alive), what do you see as your role in providing such help?

Research Navigator Guide: Social Gerontology

In analyzing your findings, compare the responses of your participants whose grandparents were from the majority U.S. culture vs. those from non-English speaking ethnic minority backgrounds vs. those whose grandparents were immigrants. To what extent did each type of grandparent impart their cultural values on these adults as children?

2. Interview at least five middle-aged adults (ages 40–50) who represent the majority American culture and whose parents were not immigrants to this country, as well as five middle-aged adults who represent an ethnic minority population (e.g. African American, Latino) or whose parents immigrated to this country. Your objective is to determine if cultural differences between these two groups are reflected by their responses to the following questions:

If your parents become frail and need full-time care, what would you do? Who would make the necessary decisions and become involved in the caregiving process?

For respondents whose parents have died, ask the following question:

Did your parents ever need long-term care, and what was your role in assuring that they received such care? Who was involved in their caregiving and in decision-making about their care?

Role of Elders in Traditional Cultures

Suggested Reading

Popular

1. Stone, W. Elders come of age. *World & I,* Nov 2003, *18,* No. 11, p. 174 (*AN 11203059*).

The author discusses the "elderhood" ceremony of the Masai in East Africa. How does this ceremony differ from more traditional coming-of-age ceremonies? Describe when and how this rite of passage is celebrated. According to the article, through what stages must a Masai man pass in his development?

2. Nonoyama, H. The family and family sociology in Japan. *American Sociologist,* Fall 2000, *31,* No. 3, p. 27 (*AN 4060216*).

An overview of the history of family sociology in Japan is given in this article. The author describes the institutionalization of Japanese family structure during the second half of the nineteenth century, and discusses the changes in the Japanese family since then. What information is presented about the role of older people in the traditional Japanese family? How has this role changed in the 20th and 21st centuries?

3. Baldauf, S. Feudal lords key to Afghan peace. *Christian Science Monitor,* 12/21/2001, *94,* No. 21, p. 6 (*AN 5728913*).

This article describes tribal feudal governments in Afghanistan and the role of village elders in making government decisions. Give specific examples of ways in which village elders make decisions. What argument does the author make about the importance of including of tribal elders in decision-making at local levels?

Scholarly

1. Jackson, D., Van Winkle, N. Contemporary perspectives on American Indian elders: identity, health, and life cycle issues. *Gerontologist,* Oct. 1999, **39,** No. 5, p. 549 (*AN 2446689*).

This article reviews abstracts about traditional and contemporary issues among older American Indians that were presented at an annual meeting of the Gerontological Society of America. What end-of-life issues are presented in these abstracts, and what information is revealed about the traditional role of older American Indians?

2. Old age and support in China: The role of the state and the family. *International Journal of Aging & Human Development,* 1999, *49,* No. 3, p. 197 (*AN 2787335*).

The relationship between social support and the well-being of older people in China is discussed. According to this article, what role do the family and state play in supporting older people? What does this information reveal about the traditional role of older people in China?

3. Poska, A. Gender, property, and retirement strategies in early modern northwestern Spain. *Journal of Family History,* Jul 2000, *25,* No. 3, p. 313 (*AN 3351191*).

The role of older women in early modern rural Spain is examined. According to this author, older women were influential in determining family economies and their own care in later life. In what ways did older women exercise this influence in determining their own future and the future of their families?

Applied Research Exercises

1. Based on your understanding of the readings above and Chapter 2, compare the role of elders in at least *three* different societies (e.g. Japan, American Indian, European countries). These can be contemporary or historic cultures. Make a list of roles played by elders, both in the family and in the larger society. To what extent do these roles differ across cultures? What are some similarities across cultures? What do these roles illustrate about the relative power, independence, and respect given to elders in these societies?

2. The gerontological literature is lacking in comparative studies of elders in different cultures. This exercise is designed to give you an opportunity to design an anthropological study that will answer more directly the questions raised in #1 above. Select *three* different cultures for this comparison, indicating why you would study them specifically. Design the study so you could obtain data directly in those countries and/or cultural groups. Indicate how you would collect data and from whom, in order to answer the same questions in each group on the following issues:

   a. definition of "elder" or "old"

   b. societal expectations of elders' work and retirement activities

   c. societal expectations of elders' roles in their families, villages, and community

The Social Consequences of Physical Aging

Anti-Aging

Suggested Reading

Popular

1. Kolata, G. Chasing youth, many gamble on hormones. *New York Times,* December 22, 2002.

This article discusses the use of human growth hormone injections as a means of counteracting the decrease in human growth hormone that occurs as a natural part of the aging process. What evidence supports the use of human growth hormone as an anti-aging technique, and what evidence is lacking? Why might it be problematic to approach aging as though it were a disease?

2. Cole, T. R., Thompson, B. Anti-aging: Are you for it or against it? *Generations, 2002, 25,* No. 4.

The guest editors of this issue—devoted entirely to a discussion of anti-aging ideas—introduce articles by scientists, scholars, and physicians who have written from their various disciplines and perspectives for this issue of *Generations.* Select two articles in this issue, summarize each and include several reasons why you agree/disagree with the ideas put forth by the authors.

3. Wade, N. Why we die, why we live: A new theory on aging. *New York Times,* July 15, 2003.

The author examines a new theory of aging proposed by Dr. Ronald Lee, UC Berkeley. The classic theory explains aging in terms of natural selection and fertility through the life cycle. Dr. Lee states that parental care should be factored in throughout the life cycle. Discuss his theory in terms of the interconnection between fertility, mortality and parental care.

Scholarly

1. Banks, D. A., Fossel, M. Telomeres, cancer and aging. *JAMA (Journal of the American Medical Association),* 1997, *278,* No. 16.

Since this article was written more than five years ago, there have been numerous studies on telomeres. In very general terms expand on how manipulating the length of telomeres can alter the life span of human cells.

2. Olshansky, S. J., Hayflick, L., Carnes, B. A. No truth to the fountain of youth. *Scientific American,* 2002, *286,* No. 6 (*AN 6630415*).

The authors contend that aging is the accumulation of random damage to the building blocks of life; these changes ultimately surpass the body's self-repair capabilities. The authors challenge many current anti-aging interventions, such as the use of antioxidants and hormone replacement therapy and discuss the irony of the escalation of an anti-aging industry. Discuss the authors' discussion of genetic research that might lead to aging interventions; include two other studies that support or refute the role of genetics as the single most reliable intervention to the aging process. Be sure to include the article, "Anti-aging Technology and Pseudoscience," (*AN 6676014*).

3. Weinert, B., Timiras, P. Invited review: Theories of aging. *Journal of Applied Physiology,* 2003, *95:* 1706–1716.

In this article the authors state: "Biological, epidemiologic, and demographic data have generated a number of theories that attempt to identify a cause or process to explain aging and its inevitable consequence, death. However, in recent years, the search for a single cause of aging, such as a single gene or the decline of a key body system, has been replaced by the view of aging as an extremely complex, multifactorial process." Discuss two other theories described in Chapter 3 that speculate on factors that shape the life span.

Research Navigator Guide: Social Gerontology

Applied Research Exercises

1. The only thing that retards aging is caloric restriction, contends Roy Walford, Professor of Pathology at UCLA, School of Medicine. His theory is that the less food you eat, the fewer free radicals you will have wreaking havoc on your genes. Discuss the debate among scientists on the pros and cons of caloric restriction in humans.

2. Aging is now being viewed as an extremely complex multifactorial process, replacing the earlier search for a single cause. There are multiple mechanisms that regulate aging at the molecular, cellular and systemic levels. Discuss why this approach to studying the aging process may help or hinder our understanding of normal aging and efforts to improve healthy aging. Use the following issue of *The Gerontologist* as a background for your discussion: *The Gerontologist* 2000 (Special Issue) 40, *(AN 3724185)*.

Caloric Restriction

Suggested Reading

Popular

1. Hochman, D. Food for holiday thought: Eat less, live to 140? *New York Times,* November 23, 2003.

This article focuses on one individual's experience with caloric restriction as a means of lengthening his life span. How does the article explain the effect of caloric restriction on longevity? What positive and negative physical and psychological effects did caloric restriction cause for the man discussed in this article?

2. Sherr, L. Eat less, live longer? Some hope cutting calories will add years to their lives. *ABC News,* December 5, 2003.

The effect of caloric restriction on quality of life and longevity is discussed. The article acknowledges the possibility that caloric restriction could increase the lifespan, but also presents some negative effects of following a calorie-restricted diet. What are some examples of these social or psychological drawbacks related to caloric restriction presented in this article?

3. Wade, N. Study spurs hope of finding way to increase human life. *New York Times,* August 25, 2003.

This article discusses the possibility that a natural substance called resveratrol could mimic the effects of caloric restriction and increase longevity in humans. Where is resveratrol found? Briefly describe the effect of caloric restriction that this substance mimics.

Scholarly

1. Downey, M., Low-calorie longevity. *Better Nutrition,* 2002, *64,* No. 12, p. 39 (*AN 8608761*).

The benefits of caloric restriction as it relates to theories of aging are discussed. List the experiments conducted on caloric restriction as presented in this article, and the benefits of caloric restriction, according to the author.

2. Finch, C., Longo, V., Evolutionary medicine: From dwarf model systems to healthy centenarians? *Science,* 2003, *299,* No. 5611, p. 1342 (*AN 9267123*).

The authors cite research with animals that found caloric restriction to be effective in increasing longevity. What practical suggestions does this article offer for preventing diseases related to aging?

3. Roth, G., Lane, M., Ingram, D., Mattison, J., Elahi, D., Tobin, J., Muller, D., Metter, E., Biomarkers of caloric restriction may predict longevity in humans. *Science,* 2002, 297, No. 5582, p. 811 (*AN 7230648*).

The authors imply that caloric restriction is highly effective in slowing aging in animals, and discuss why research findings with rodents could be relevant to humans. What results are discussed in this article to support the idea that caloric restriction is an effective method for slowing aging?

Applied Research Exercises

1. Conduct an informal survey with at least 10 men and 10 women in their 20s regarding their attitudes about caloric restriction and longevity. Ask each person if they would be willing to reduce their daily food intake to about 1500 calories, and to restrict the types of foods that could be consumed (using guidelines from the articles above), if they knew with some certainty that this would extend their lifespan. What level of caloric restriction would they accept, and for how long, in order to extend their lifespan? Does your research show differences by gender and lifestyle?

2. To what extent can studies of rodents and other animals lead to useful guidelines for human studies in the future? After reading the articles above, design an "ideal" study (although it may not be practically feasible) that you could use to test the long-term benefits of caloric restriction. What specific levels of calories and types of food would you use in this study, and how long would the study last? At what age would human subjects be enrolled in this study?

Stem Cell Research

Suggested Reading

Popular

1. France-Presse, A. Lab successes revive hopes for stem cell transplants. *New York Times,* June 20, 2002.

The author identifies research advances on how to grow stem cells in order to make replacement tissues for organs killed by disease. The article also discusses the difference between using embryonic stem cells and stem cells from adults. What are the advantages of using embryonic stem cells for treating various debilitating diseases, and what ethical questions surround this kind of research?

2. The Associated Press. California law permits stem cell research. *New York Times,* September 23, 2002.

This article reports on the recent passage of a California law allowing stem cell research from fetal and embryonic tissue. According to the article, what are some examples of medical conditions that could benefit from stem cell research? What are the arguments against stem cell research presented in this article?

3. Wade, N., Scientists make 2 stem cell advances. *New York Times,* June 21, 2002.

The focus of this article is on two advances made in cell therapy research as an alternative to drug use, and the relationship between the science of stem cell research and politics surrounding the issue. What are the two advances in cell therapy research discussed in this article, and what are the political arguments against these advances?

Scholarly

1. Holden, C. Stem cells show versatility, power. *Science Now,* 2002, p. 1 (*AN 7018571*).

The author summarizes two studies regarding stem cell research. Describe these two studies as they relate to the harvesting of cells from bone marrow, and the treatment of Parkinson's disease with stem cells.

2. Lo, B., Chou, V., Cedars, M., Gates, E. Taylor, R., Wagner, R., Wolf, L., Yamamoto, K., Consent from donors for embryo and stem cell research. *Science,* 2003, *301,* No. 5635, p. 921 (*AN 10691308*).

In this article, the authors focus on the importance of obtaining informed consent in studies related to stem cell research. Discuss why informed consent is important for any type of research, and how consenting to participate in stem cell research differs from the informed consent process in other types of research.

3. McCarthy, Michael, Two new studies likely to add fire to stem cell debate. *Lancet,* 2002, *359* No. 9324, p. 2171 (*AN 6850257*).

The results from two studies on stem cells and the debate surrounding their findings are discussed. What was found about the versatility of mouse bone marrow stem cells versus embryonic stem cells, and how do these findings affect the future of stem cell research?

Applied Research Exercises

1. After reading the popular and scientific articles describing recent findings of researchers studying stem cells, list the diseases for which this technique may have some promise. Indicate whether both embryonic and adult stem cells have been found to be effective for the disease, if this is evident from the research reports. Then conduct an informal survey of young and middle-aged adults regarding their knowledge about these techniques.

2. Conduct an informal survey of adults who are not in the field of medicine to obtain their attitudes on:
   a. whether stem cell research should be funded by the federal government;
   b. whether stem cells should be obtained from embryos, why or why not;
   c. whether stem cells should be obtained from adults, why or why not;
   d. what conditions should be met before an individual should undergo stem cell transplants.

Research Navigator Guide: Social Gerontology

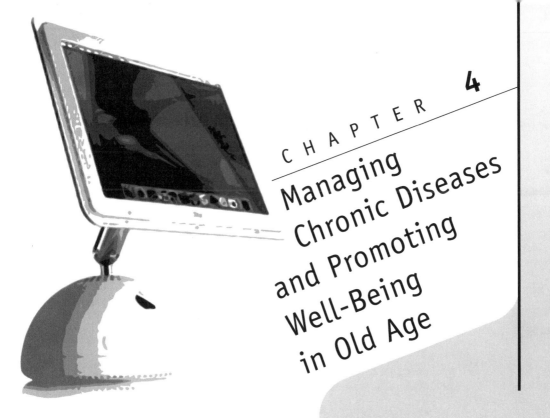

CHAPTER 4

Managing Chronic Diseases and Promoting Well-Being in Old Age

Preventing and Treating Osteoporosis

Suggested Reading

Popular

1. Brody, J. Options for protecting bones after menopause. *New York Times,* April 22, 2003.

The author describes a study in which women stopped taking estrogen in order to protect their heart and breast health, but also experienced a loss of bone as a result. What dietary advice does the author give for young people to prevent against osteoporosis in later life? What non-hormonal options are available for the treatment and prevention of osteoporosis for post-menopausal women?

2. Reuters. Annual injection may stop osteoporosis. *New York Times,* February 28, 2002.

A study is presented that focused on the use of an annual injection of zoledronic acid as a way to treat osteoporosis. The study suggests that this drug, when administered as an injection, is effective in blocking brittleness in bones. What is the benefit of this kind of treatment? What does the author suggest is the main flaw in this study?

3. The Associated Press. FDA approves new osteoporosis therapy, a bone-growing drug. *New York Times,* November 27, 2002

This article reports the approval by the FDA of *teriparatide,* a new drug created for the treatment of osteoporosis that works by stimulating bone growth in older adults. According to this article, how does this drug differ from others used in the way it treats osteoporosis? What are possible risks involved in the use of *teriparatide?*

Scholarly

1. Capriotti, T. Pharmacologic prevention and treatment of osteoporosis in women. *MEDSURG Nursing,* 2000, *9* No. 2, p. 86 (*AN 3177764*).

This article focuses on pharmacologic treatments in the preservation of bone strength in women with osteoporosis. What specific medications have been found to be effective in preserving bone strength, and what supplements does the author suggest for preventing osteoporosis?

2. Solomon, C. Bisphosphonates and osteoporosis. *New England Journal of Medicine,* 2002, *346* No. 9, p. 642 (*AN 6183667*).

The author presents information about the use of bisphosphonates to treat osteoporosis in post-menopausal women. What are the effects of bisphosphonates on the risk of fracture, and what issues need to be studied further in order to use bisphosphonates more effectively?

3. Turkoski, B. Treating osteoporosis without hormones. *Orthopaedic Nursing,* 2002, *21,* No. 5, p. 80 (*AN 7584926*).

Debates surrounding the use of hormone replacement therapy (HRT) to prevent osteoporosis are discussed. The author presents risks of HRT and gives alternatives for preventing osteoporosis. What are the risks of HRT and what are some approved pharmaceutical alternatives presented by the author?

Applied Research Exercises

1. Conduct an informal survey with at least 10 women under age 40 and 10 who are age 55 and older, **and** who are postmenopausal. Ask each woman what she knows about osteoporosis and how she can prevent it. Probe what they know about medications, supplements, diet, and exercise to prevent osteoporosis. To what extent is each woman using these techniques to prevent this condition? Are there differences between the two groups based on their age and/or menopausal status?

Which group seems most aware of the most recent research as evidenced by the articles above?

2. Review the articles above to determine what age groups have been tested with the medications and supplements that are described. To what extent are these groups representative of the populations who are most at risk for osteoporosis (i.e. in terms of ethnicity, age, and gender)? What other groups should be considered, given the risk of osteoporosis for specific segments of the population as described in Chapters 4 and 15?

Health Promotion for Disadvantaged Elders

Suggested Reading

Popular

1. Gorman, C. Why so many of us are getting diabetes, *Time Magazine,* November 30, 2003.

This article identifies new developments in the detection and prevention of Type 2 diabetes. After reviewing this article, discuss what scientists have learned about the prevention of this disease and its complications.

2. O'Neil, J. Prevention: Problems at the medicine chest, *New York Times,* January 1, 2003.

The author highlights a study reporting that many women who should be taking medicine to prevent heart disease are not doing so. Specifically, what does this article suggest about health behaviors of postmenopausal women who have experienced heart problems in the past?

3. Hawthorne, F. With the increase in Type 2 diabetes comes a focus on its warning signs. *New York Times,* June 22, 2003.

Early detection and treatment of Type 2 diabetes are discussed. What are some factors that contribute to this chronic condition, and what are some of its warning signs?

Scholarly

1. Buijs, R. et al. "Promoting participation: Evaluation of a health promotion program for low income seniors. *Journal of Community Health Nursing,* Summer 2003, *20,* No. 2 (*AN 9916795*).

The authors describe program interventions delivered in elders' apartment buildings, including exercise classes, health information sessions and newsletters. The authors examine how and why the program worked in these settings. Discuss how such an approach to health promotion might be applied to other populations of older adults. To what extent is this a cost-effective method of providing health promotion?

2. Angel, R. J., Angel, J. L., Markides, K. S., Stability and change in health insurance among older Mexican Americans: Longitudinal evidence from the Hispanic established populations for epidemiologic study of the elderly, *American Journal of Public Health,* Aug 2002, *92* No. 8, p. 1264 (*AN 7069703*).

This study examined health insurance coverage and its relationship to levels of health and receipt of care in older Mexican Americans. Because it describes the status of a large, representative sample of older Mexican Americans, it provides valuable data on their ability to afford health insurance. Based on the findings presented in this article, discuss the vulnerabilities among older Mexican Americans due to lack of private supplemental coverage.

3. Boyce, W. F., Disadvantaged persons' participation in health promotion projects: Some structural dimensions. *Social Science and Medicine,* 2001, *52*, No. 10, p. 1551 (*AN 4683289*).

This article discusses projects in the Canadian Health Promotion Contribution Program that examine participation by disadvantaged elders in health promotion projects. What structural factors are identified that might influence the participation of poor women or persons with disabilities in health promotion projects?

Applied Research Exercises

1. Design a community-based health promotion program for older people who live in low-income housing:
   - How will you decide what topics should be included?
   - How will you encourage participation by elders who would most benefit from health promotion activities but are reluctant?
2. Research on managing chronic diseases such as diabetes and hypertension has consistently shown that health promotion programs lasting a few weeks have many short-term benefits, but these benefits fade after a few months. What are some techniques that could be used to sustain beneficial outcomes such as keeping blood glucose levels or cholesterol levels low after an exercise or diet intervention? How could you assure that the older adult continues to benefit from these health promotion efforts years after the intervention ends?

Research Navigator Guide: Social Gerontology

Chronic Illness

Suggested Reading

Popular

1. Doughton, S. Stakes high to help those with chronic diseases. *The Seattle Times,* November 11, 2003.

This article discusses the chronic-care model, which focuses on the management of chronic diseases. The article points out that many people are receiving less than adequate care for chronic diseases because of high health care and medication costs. Give three examples of ways in which the proposed chronic-care model serves to provide better care at a lower cost.

2. Kolata, G. Is frailty inevitable? Some experts say no. *New York Times,* November 19, 2002.

The definition and causes of frailty are explored in this article. List at least three characteristics that an older person might have in order to be called "frail". What biological factors are being studied in connection with frailty? To what extent are these inevitable or preventable?

3. Marino, V. Pharmaceutical research is focusing on the elderly. *New York Times,* June 30, 2002.

The sale of pharmaceutical drugs to older people with chronic illnesses is discussed. What problems can arise from companies' targeting older people directly for pharmaceutical sales in order to maintain their corporate revenues?

Scholarly

1. Cuijpers, P., Lammeren, P. Depressive symptoms in chronically ill elderly people in residential homes. *Aging & Mental Health,* Aug 99, *3,* No. 3, p. 221 (*AN 3954758*).

The authors examine the relationship between depression and chronic illness in older people living in residential homes. What does this article indicate about the relationship between depressive symptoms and chronic illness? What were some limitations of this study and how might they have affected the results?

2. Gooberman-Hill, R. Alvis, S., Ebrahim, S. Understanding long-standing illness among older people. *Social Science & Medicine,* Jun 2003, *56,* No. 12, p. 2555 (*AN 9722495*).

Research Navigator Guide: Social Gerontology

This article discusses surveys about long-standing illness, infirmity, or disability in older people that are used in planning services. What affects older people's descriptions of their own health status? What does this article suggest about the use of questionnaire-based surveys for measuring chronic illness?

3. Hodges, H., Keeley, A., Grier, E. Masterworks of art and chronic illness experiences in the elderly. *Journal of Advanced Nursing,* Nov 2001, *36,* No. 3, p. 389 (*AN 5310742*).

A unique approach to studying perceptions of chronic disease among registered nurses and nursing students is described in this article. The researchers used masterworks of art as a method of examining this group's perceptions about caring for chronically ill older persons. How did these groups differ in their perceptions? Explain the paradox of inertia-movement in chronically ill older persons, as described in this article.

Applied Research Exercises

1. Interview at least 10 adults aged 55 and older who have been coping with one or more chronic diseases, such as diabetes, hypertension, and heart disease. Ask them to describe *how long* they have been dealing with the chronic condition, *what* they have been doing to *manage it,* and *to what extent it affects their activities of daily living* (using activities included in ADL measures such as those described in Chapter 4).

2. Review at least three popular magazines (e.g. *Time, Newsweek, Readers' Digest*), examining at least six issues in the past year. Make a list of ads by drug companies aimed at people with chronic diseases (e.g. hypertension, diabetes), the name of each drug, the audience to which it is directed (e.g. older women, African American elders), and how the drug is presented as a treatment for that particular condition. Discuss the similarities or differences across the different magazines in the ads and how they are presented.

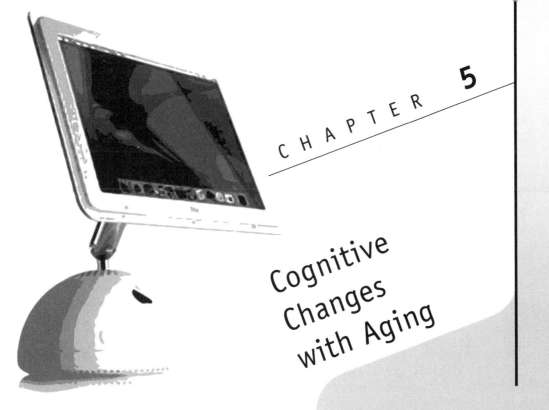

CHAPTER 5

Cognitive Changes with Aging

Lifelong Learning

Suggested Reading

Popular

1. DeGrolama, J. Retirees: The 'New Kids' on Campus. *USA Today Magazine,* July 2003, *132,* No. 2698 *(AN 1020821).*

The author discusses issues related to education in the U.S. Many colleges are making an effort to bridge the gap between traditional-aged students and older adults who are returning to school. Describe what universities might do to attract older people to participate in life-long learning.

2. Liebert, M. A. Life-long learning opportunities for seniors on the web. *Cyberpsychology and Behavior,* No 6 website: www.liebertpub.com/

This article points out the wide variety of educational opportunities and resources offered to older adults on the web. Discuss the drawbacks and benefits of online education for older people.

3. Schembri, A. Educating the elderly: Universities of the third age. *Bold,* Vol. 4 No. 4.

The experiences of a University of the Third Age (U3A) program in Malta are described. The program was developed to offer educational and life-long learning opportunities for older persons. The program organizes educational, academic and cultural activities among elders, encouraging them to utilize their own wealth of experiences for their self-fulfillment and for the education of others. Compare the U3A programs in Malta; Prague, Czechoslovakia; Cambridge, England; and Toulouse, France.

Scholarly

1. Aylward, S., Stolee, P, Keat, N., Johncox, V. Effectiveness of continuing education in long-term care: A literature review. *The Gerontologist,* 2003, *43,* No. 2 (*AN 9514987*).

The authors examine the effectiveness of continuing education programs that are offered to staff in long-term care facilities. Discuss the factors that affect the ability of long-term care employees to implement new learning.

2. Schulz, J. H. "Full Monty" and life-long learning in the 21st century. *Journal of Aging and Social Policy,* 2000, *11,* No. 2–3, p. 71–82.

This article addresses the issue of what government can do to retrain older workers. Identify why this is important and any examples of training and employment programs that you know as having successfully assisted older workers.

3. Bronte, L. Learning to change: the hallmark of a long lifetime. *Adult Learning,* 1997 Vol. 8 No. 5–6, p. 11–13.

The author discusses how education has traditionally been focused on the young. Since the 1950s when life expectancy began to increase significantly, there has been a growth in programs for adult learners. Identify the three different patterns of career change described in this article, and elaborate on why the need to continue growing and developing is a deeply rooted drive in humans.

Applied Research Exercises

1. In his book, *Lifelong learning in action: transforming education in the 21st century,* Norman Longworth describes how continuing education influences ways of life and thinking in today's society. Discuss with at least *three* people over the age of 50 what they have done to continue their own education during middle age. What formal and informal programs have they participated in, with the goal of continuing their life-long education? If they have not done anything, ask why not.

Research Navigator Guide: Social Gerontology

2. Assume you are an administrator at a local community college in charge of lifelong learning. Using the concepts you have learned in this chapter and in the selected articles in *Content Select,* design a model program that would be most beneficial to "older learners," i.e. age 60+. Explain *why* you would select various options, such as on-campus vs. in-community vs. electronic learning; a self-paced vs. group timeline; and types of courses that would be best for these formats and this audience.

Tip-of-the-Tongue Phenomenon

Suggested Reading

Popular

1. Crawford, K. G. Somers, M. Y Sparkman, A. D. The effects of cues and number of items learned on the tip-of-the-tongue-phenomenon. University of Florida, on the website: http://www.psych.ufl.edu/~levy/96_6.htm

Discuss the researchers' methods, results and discussions on tip-of-the-tongue issues.

2. Bower, B. A tip of the tongue to the brain. *Science News,* Sept. 8, 2001, *160,* No. 10 *(AN 5142364).*

Researchers have identified several brain areas that together underlie the experience of feeling certain that a piece of forgotten information is nonetheless on the tip of one's tongue. Discuss localization of specific cognitive functions in the brain that may affect this phenomenon.

3. Explain in detail the difference between normal word-finding problems in older persons and those with Alzheimer's disease. See the website on memory: http://www.memory-key.com/Seniors/wordfinding_in_age.htm#Older

Scholarly

1. Burke, M. M., MacKay, D. G., Worthley, J. A. & Wade, E. On the tip of the tongue: What causes word-finding failures in young and older adults? *Journal of Memory and Language,* 2003, *30,* p. 542–579.

The authors note that tip-of-the-tongue (TOTs) experiences increase as we age. Discuss why the increase in memory failures applies to names of people and objects in our immediate environment, yet not to abstract words. Explain why "pop-ups" are more common for adults.

2. James, L. S., Burke, D. M. Phonological priming effects on word retrieval and *tip-of-the-tongue* experiences in young and older adults. *Journal of Experimental Psychology/Learning, Memory & Cognition,* 2000, *26* No. 6 *(AN 3932920).*

The authors cite other studies that demonstrated that TOTs are a hallmark of old age, increasing in frequency with normal aging in both experimental and naturalistic studies *(A. S. Brown & Nix, 1996; Burke et al., 1991; Cohen & Faulkner, 1986; Heine, Ober, & Shenaut, 1999; Maylor, 1990b; Rastle & Burke, 1996)* and ranking as older adults' most annoying cognitive failure *(Lovelace & Twohig, 1990).* What are some factors that led the researchers to conclude that TOTs are normal and not a sign of dementia?

3. White, K. K., Abrams, L. Does priming specific syllables during tip-of-the-tongue states facilitate word retrieval in older adults? *Psychology & Aging,* 2002, *17,* No. 2 *(AN 6806783).*

In order to learn to read, a person must be aware of phonemes—the smallest functional unit of sound. For example, the word "cat" contains three distinctly different sounds. Discuss the effect of phonological priming of specific syllables on TOT resolution in old age.

Applied Research Exercises

1. Discuss what techniques you have used and have observed other people use in order to overcome tip-of-the-tongue experiences. Which techniques are more or less effective?
2. Design a program that can help healthy older adults who complain of increasing tip-of-the-tongue experiences, working with them to improve their problems with TOTs. For the purposes of this exercise, focus on name recall ability.

Wisdom

Suggested Reading

Popular

1. Morris, B. R. The body may creak, but the brains hum along. *New York Times,* March 12, 2002.

The author looks at the lives of four well-known octogenarians, still working, who have achieved, in their eyes, a specific wisdom. Summarize the working lives and outlooks of these four older people and tell in your own words why you think they have attained wisdom.

2. Life begins at 80. *Education,* Summer 2000, *120,* No. 4 (*AN 3365071*).

This article asserts that life begins at 80. Discuss this theory and why you do or do not agree with the theory.

3. Nagourney, E. Aging: Brain boosts, from the other side. *New York Times,* Nov. 19, 2002.

Older adults who draw on both sides of the brain seem to do better at some mental tasks than those who use just one side, a new study in the journal *Neuro Image* reports. Give examples of three more activities that may show enhanced mental acuity in the later years.

Scholarly

1. Ardelt, M. Intellectual versus wisdom-related knowledge: The case for a different kind of learning in the later years of life. *Educational Gerontology,* 2000, *26,* No. 6 (*AN 4140568*).

The author illustrates the difference between intellectual and wisdom-related knowledge and argues that wisdom is crucial for aging well. Compare and contrast knowledge and wisdom throughout a person's life.

2. Baltes, P. B., Staudinger, U. M. Wisdom. *American Psychologist,* 2002, *55,* No. 1 (*AN 908573*).

The authors discuss the seven properties of wisdom. Explain the authors' five conclusions about this concept. How would you test for each of these elements of wisdom?

3. McKee, P., Barber, C. On defining wisdom. *International Journal of Aging & Human Development,* 1999, *49,* No. 2 (*AN 2714503*).

The article examines the psychological and social studies of aging and the aged. The authors give classical definitions of wisdom and explain the link between wisdom, illusion and temptation. Give some examples of cases where these concepts may be missed.

Applied Research Exercises

1. Behavioral scientists are finding good news about the prospects for successful aging as they delve ever more deeply into the science of wisdom. The best news of all seems to be that people can work toward achieving wisdom, that it is not a "gift" bestowed on a few selected people. Discuss the types of activities you can do if you wanted to work toward "growing wise" in your old age. For some examples of this, see: Baltes, P. B. Baltes, M. M. Harvesting the fruits of age: growing older, growing wise. *Science & Spirit* 1999 Vol. 10, p. 12–14.

2. Research by Baltes and Staudinger (see #2 above) suggests that aging is not synonymous with achieving wisdom. Consider the lives of three people you know personally who are age 60 or older, or three public figures (in politics, entertainment, etc.) whose lives you have read about. In what ways would you say these three people have or have not achieved wisdom, using definitions of wisdom used in the readings from *Content Select* or in Chapter 5.

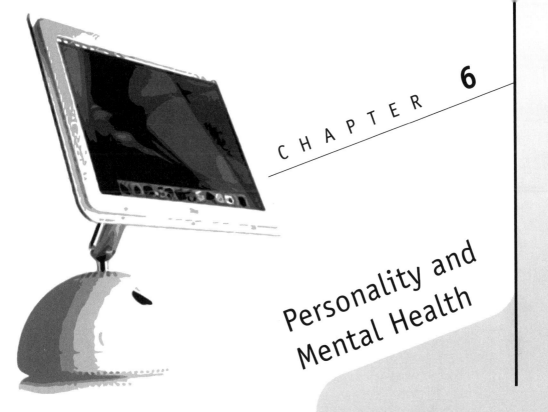

Personality and Mental Health

Early Detection of Dementia

Suggested Reading

Popular

1. Kolata, G. An early sign of Alzheimer's brings fear, and new insight. *New York Times,* June 2, 2002.

2. Kolata, G. New ideas energize Alzheimer's battle, *New York Times,* January 14, 2003.

This article presents a new hypothesis about the cause of Alzheimer's disease and discusses the importance of early detection for treatment. Whereas the disease has generally been treated based on the assumption that it is caused by the death of brain cells, this article suggests that the disease might be related to the interruption of signals between living and dying cells. If this is the case, what possible early treatment strategies are presented in this article?

3. Wellbery, C. Repetitive behaviors: A clue to early dementia. *American Family Physician,* 2003, *68,* No. 2, p. 371 (*AN 10380085*).

The author discusses a study that investigated forgetfulness and symptoms that help in the early detection and diagnosis of dementia. According to this study, what symptoms might be a sign that a person is experiencing the early signs of dementia? What does this suggest for the early detection of Alzheimer's disease?

Scholarly

1. Fountoulakis, K., Fotiou, F., Lacovides, A., Kaprinis, G. Do depressive patients with family history of dementia constitute a separate group? A case report study. *International Journal of Psychiatry in Clinical Practice,* 2000, *4,* No. 3 (*AN 4430542*).

A study is described that examined the relationship between depression and family history of dementia with the development of Alzheimer's disease. The authors conclude that there is limited data to support a connection between depression, family history of dementia, and the development of Alzheimer's disease. In what ways does this study support or refute the possibility of using patient and family health characteristics to provide early detection of Alzheimer's?

2. Mackinnon, A., Mulligan, R., Combining cognitive testing and informant report to increase accuracy in screening for dementia. *American Journal of Psychiatry,* 1998, *155,* No. 11, p. 1529 (*AN 1255184*).

This article discusses the benefits of combining cognitive testing with an informant report questionnaire in the diagnosis of dementia. Discuss the findings of the study, and whether this may increase accuracy in dementia screening. In your review of the article, note how graphical methods used in this report can be applied to individual cases.

3. Villareal, D., Morris, J. The Diagnosis of Alzheimer's Disease. *Journal of Alzheimer's Disease,* 1999, *1,* No. 4/5, p. 249 (*AN 4832886*).

Given the importance of early diagnosis of dementia, the authors suggest that the best approach for detecting these disorders is through a clinical examination that focuses on the patient's declining cognitive abilities. According to the authors, why is clinical examination so effective? What role do biological markers play in the detection of dementia?

Applied Research Exercises

1. Based on the articles summarized above, and the more extensive discussion of research on dementia described in Chapter 6, prepare a list of possible predictors of Alzheimer's disease. Can these predictors be readily measured or assessed by observation or by existing tests, or will it be necessary to develop new tests? How would you use this information to develop a battery of tests to detect Alzheimer's disease in its earliest stages?

2. Present a rationale for offering older adults and their families a diagnostic test for Alzheimer's disease, Pick's disease, vascular dementia, or other types of irreversible dementias. What are some reasons why it may not be in the patient's best interest to offer early detection options, including any ethical issues of concern.

Maintaining a Healthy Outlook with Aging

Suggested Reading

Popular

1. The Associated Press, We're getting older, better: Study links happy outlook, longer life, *The Seattle Times,* May 8, 2001.

This article discusses practical implications of the Nun Study (described in more detail in Chapter 6), and suggests that a positive emotional state can help in fighting disease and living a longer life. What were some specific characteristics of the nuns who lived longer, and how did these differ from the health, intellectual, and social activities of nuns who developed Alzheimer's disease?

2. Dreifus, C. Taking a clinical look at human emotions. *New York Times,* October 8, 2002.

The focus of this article is on a study of synapses in the brain as a means of understanding processes such as thinking, perception, memory, and ultimately, human emotion. The author suggests that synapses are wired according to our genes and our individual experiences, and thus, they play a key role in understanding emotion. According to the article, why is this information considered a breakthrough? Why is it useful to study emotion based on what the article calls "the quantifiable aspects of the mind"?

3. Duenwald, M. Power of positive thinking extends, it seems, to aging, *New York Times,* November 19, 2002.

Studies that have focused on the relationship between personality and longevity are reviewed, offering some evidence that people who have a positive outlook on aging tend to live longer. According to the article, what characteristics of an optimistic outlook might contribute to longevity?

Scholarly

1. Duberstein, P. R., Sorensen, S., Lyness, J. M., King, D. A., Conwell, Y., Seidlitz, L., Caine, E. D. Personality is associated with perceived health and functional status in older primary care patients. *Psychology & Aging,* Mar 2003, *18,* No. 1, p. 25; (*AN 9336042*).

Research is described that examined the association between personality characteristics in older adults and their perceived health and functional status. Briefly summarize the methodology and results of the study.

2. Pushkar, D., Reis, M., Morros, M. Motivation, personality and well-being in older volunteers, *International Journal of Aging & Human Development,* Jun 2002, *55,* No. 2, p. 141 (*AN 8881815*).

The authors studied older volunteers and the relationship between their personality traits and well-being. The study suggests that specific personality traits can result in better mental health outcomes in old age than others. What steps were used in carrying out this study, and how can people learn to adapt in order to achieve well-being as they age?

3. Saveman, B. I. The significance of personality factors for various dimensions of life quality among older people, *Aging & Mental Health,* May 2002, *6,* No. 2, p. 178 (*AN 6687623*).

This researcher examined the relationship between personality and quality of life in old age. Choose three personality traits discussed in this article, and explain what the study suggests is the effect of each trait on different aspects of quality of life.

Applied Research Exercises

1. Interview a group of 20–40 year-olds about how they envision themselves in their 70s and 80s. To what extent do they see their personality traits and styles of coping today affecting how they adapt to events they will experience in their later years? Can they identify any personality traits and coping styles that may help them avoid some of the psychological disorders of aging such as depression?

2. Interview a group of healthy 60–80 year-olds whom you would describe as having aged with good mental health. As them how they view their lives and the ways in which their personality traits have helped them achieve active aging and avoid psychological disorders as they reached their later years.

Treating Mental Disorders in Old Age

Suggested Reading

Popular

1. Nagourney, E. Aging: Mild depression and eroding immunity. *New York Times,* February 12, 2002.

This article suggests that depression in older people may be related to the strength of their immune systems. How do researchers suggest that depression can weaken the immune system, and what treatments do they recommend in order to reduce this interactive effect?

2. Pear, R. In a first, Medicare coverage is authorized for Alzheimer's. *New York Times,* March 31, 2002.

Medicare coverage for treatment of Alzheimer's disease is discussed, reflecting studies that show that Alzheimer's patients benefit from certain kinds of treatment. List three different ways in which Medicare coverage of Alzheimer's treatment affects the lives and families of Alzheimer's patients.

3. Tuller, D. Race is on for a pill to save the memory. *New York Times,* July 29, 2003.

This article discusses the use of drugs in Alzheimer's patients that are aimed at treating memory loss. Give an example of one type of drug described in this article that might be used to treat memory loss, and explain how it would work.

Scholarly

1. Ashaye, O., Livingston, G., Orrell, M. Does standardized needs assessment improve the outcome of psychiatric day hospital care for older people? A randomized controlled trial. *Aging & Mental Health,* May 2003, 7, No. 3, p. 195 (*AN 9930321*).

This article addresses the effectiveness of assessment techniques in psychiatric day hospitals for older people. What differences were found between the Care Programme Approach (CPA) and the Camberwell Assessment of Need for the Elderly (CANE)? What effect do these assessment techniques have in providing care for older people with mental health problems?

2. Beck-Little, R., The use of Reminiscence Therapy for the treatment of depression in rural-dwelling older adults. *Issues in Mental Health Nursing,* Apr 2002, *23*, No. 3, p. 279 (*AN 6373616*).

Research Navigator Guide: Social Gerontology

This article explores the use of reminiscence therapy as treatment for depression among institutionalized older adults. What is reminiscence therapy and why might it be a more appropriate treatment option than traditional methods for individuals living in rural areas?

3. Stek, M., van Exel, E., van Tilburg, W., Beekman, A. The prognosis of depression in old age: outcome six to eight years after clinical treatment. *Aging & Mental Health,* Aug 2002, *6,* No. 3, p. 282 (*AN 7175379*).

This study examined the prognosis of hospitalized elderly patients with depressive disorder, and the effectiveness of clinical treatment. List some predictors of outcomes in clinically treated elderly discussed in this article.

Applied Research Exercises

1. Based on the articles summarized above and the readings in Chapter 6, make a list of medical conditions that may be triggered or aggravated by depression in older adults. Based on this knowledge about the links between depression and some systemic conditions, design a treatment program for older persons with clinical symptoms of depression. Indicate how you would assess the impact of treatment for depression on this condition and on any medical conditions the older person may have. You can use multiple modes of therapy, but be sure to justify each approach you use, based on the research findings described in the articles listed above and in the description of depression and its treatment in Chapter 6.

2. Based on the articles summarized above and the discussion of psychiatric disorders in Chapter 6, describe the current status of assessing treatment outcomes for depression and dementia. What are some problems inherent to such assessment for older persons in particular?

CHAPTER 7

Love, Intimacy, and Sexuality in Old Age

Herbal Supplements and Alternative Therapies for Menopause

Suggested Reading

Popular

1. Berger, L. Common sense for cooling down. *New York Times,* August 12, 2003.

Written in lay language, this article gives practical suggestions for dealing with menopause by using herbal supplements and maintaining a balanced lifestyle. The author emphasizes that menopause is not a disease, but a stage in life. Describe three ideas presented in this article to help women maintain a healthy lifestyle during menopause.

2. Kolata, G. Race to fill void in menopause-drug market. *New York Times,* September 1, 2002.

Alternatives to hormone therapy for menopause have been increasing, along with growing debates about estrogen replacement therapy. What specific alternatives does the author discuss and what risks might be involved in the marketing of these alternatives?

3. Nagourney, E. Remedies: In lieu of hormones: Questions. *New York Times,* November 19, 2002.

This article provides a useful review on alternatives to hormone replacement therapy for menopause, suggesting that some herbal remedies and dietary supplements are effective and some are not. According to the author, which remedies have been found to be most effective?

Scholarly

1. Is black cohosh estrogenic? *Nutrition Reviews,* 2003, *61,* No. 5, p. 83 (*AN 9846193*).

This article discusses the use of black cohosh as an alternative supplement for women who are experiencing menopausal symptoms. The paper focuses on evidence for and against the effectiveness of black cohosh as an estrogen substitute. What new data is discussed in this article that disputes the estrogenic theory about black cohosh?

2. Cutson, T., Meuleman, E., Managing menopause. *American Family Physician,* 2000, *61,* No. 5, p. 1391 (*AN 2910189*).

The authors review the literature on treating the symptoms of menopause. What psychological effects of menopause do the authors discuss? What herbal supplements do they suggest as a way to manage these side effects?

3. Morelli, V., Naquin, C., Alternative therapies for traditional disease states: menopause. *American Family Physician,* 2002, *66,* No. 1, p. 129 (*AN 6965644*).

The treatment of post-menopausal cardiovascular disease and osteoporosis are discussed in this article. What research do the authors present regarding the effect of hormone replacement therapy on osteoporosis? What evidence is there for the effects of soy and fish oil consumption on menopausal symptoms?

Applied Research Exercises

1. After reviewing the description of research and popular support for alternative herbal therapies for the symptoms of menopause in the articles listed above, what would you consider to be the most reasonable recommendations for the most common symptoms (e.g. night sweats, sleeplessness)? What recommendations would you make to women who are beginning to experience these symptoms and are unsure whether to use estrogen, combined estrogen and progesterone, or herbal remedies?

2. Conduct brief interviews with at least three women in each of three age groups: 50–55, 60–65, and 70–80. Ask each of them if they expe-

Research Navigator Guide: Social Gerontology

rienced any symptoms during the menopause, what these were, and if they took hormones or any alternative remedies to manage these symptoms. Are there differences across these cohorts and between the women in each cohort in the types of symptoms and treatments they describe?

The Meaning of Sexuality in Older Adults

Suggested Reading

Popular

1. Barnett, E. Sex therapist, 90, focuses on the elderly. *The Seattle Times,* March 12, 2000.

The author interviewed 90-year-old therapist Eleanor Hamilton, who studies sexuality in older adults, with a focus on the sexual fulfillment of women who outlive their partners. What are some aspects of what sexuality means to Eleanor Hamilton, and what new ideas has she contributed to the study of sexuality in later life?

2. Bloom, P. Sex in the elderly. *Healthology Press,* ABCNews.com, http://abcnews.go.com/sections/living/MensSexualHealth/aging_sex.html

Various aspects of sex and sexuality are explored in this article. What is the perspective used by the author to describe sexuality in older adults? What does this perspective suggest about the way sexuality is approached in popular media in the United States?

3. Old-age 'tsar' promotes sex. *BBC World News,* September 13, 2001. http://news.bbc.co.uk/1/hi/health/1541706.stm

This article suggests that financial stability and regular sex are critical factors for health and longevity. Give at least two reasons that support the assertion of this article that regular sex contributes to longer life. In what ways does this report contribute to the public perception of sexuality in older adults?

Scholarly

1. Gott, M., Hinchliff, S. How important is sex in later life? The views of older people. *Social Science & Medicine,* Apr 2003, *56,* No. 8, p. 1617 *(AN 9307886).*

The authors describe the results of a survey of older adults' attitudes toward sex in later life. They acknowledge popular, research-related, and political

Research Navigator Guide: Social Gerontology

images of sexuality, but the survey focuses on older people's attitudes toward the role and priority of sex in their own lives. What factors led participants in this study to place less importance on sex? How did perceptions of 'normal aging' affect participants' attitudes toward sex in later life?

2. Trudel, G., Turgeon, L., Piché, L. Marital and sexual aspects of old age. *Sexual & Relationship Therapy,* Nov 2000, *15,* No. 4, p. 381 (*AN 3888723*).

The literature on marital relationships and sexual functioning in older people is reviewed, with a focus on physiological and psychological factors that may influence sexual behavior. How do attitudes on sexuality affect the aging process? What intervention methods are presented in this study, and why are these methods, geared toward conjugal functioning, important for older adults?

3. Yahnke, R., Aziz, S., Baladerian, N. Sykes, J. Intimacy, sexual expression, and dementia. *Gerontologist,* Dec 2002, *42,* No. 6, p. 873, (*AN 8736555*).

This article is a review of two videos on intimacy, sexual expression, and dementia. How do these two videos express the meaning of sexuality in older adults with dementia? How are they similar or different?

Applied Research Exercises

1. Review at least three popular magazines aimed at women (e.g. *Cosmopolitan, Women's World, Ms., Working Woman*), searching for articles in the past year that address sexuality in women. What is the target group for these articles—young, middle-aged, or older women? Is there a bias in favor of one or another age group? Do you see differences among the different magazines in their audience and/or topics related to sexuality?

2. Based on your review of the above articles and Chapter 7, imagine that you are in the role of training health care providers on older adults and sexuality. Identify the recommendations that you would make to each of the following kinds of providers regarding sexuality and aging:
   - a nurse practitioner in an HMO,
   - a manager of an assisted living facility,
   - the director of nursing in a nursing home,
   - the social worker in a senior center.

Research Navigator Guide: Social Gerontology

Issues Related to Sexuality in Long-Term Care Facilities

Suggested Reading

Popular

1. Care homes 'should have rooms for sex'. *BBC News*. April 17, 2001. http://news.bbc.co.uk/1/hi/health/1281284.stm

The issue of providing separate rooms for couples in long-term care facilities is addressed, arguing that older people are not always given enough privacy because it is assumed that they are too old for sex. What does this article say about married couples in long-term care facilities? How does their ability to have privacy affect their emotional well-being?

2. King, M. Aging poses new health-care, legal challenges for gay partners. *The Seattle Times,* October 7, 2001.

This article addresses the fear of gay and lesbian couples that they would have to hide their sexual orientation if they were to live in a long-term care facility. The article presents the idea of retirement communities geared toward gay couples and individuals. What other practical ideas does the author suggest? Why is it so important to address issues facing gay and lesbian couples who are over 50 years old now? How do their generation's challenges differ from younger gays and lesbians?

3. Kirchofer, T. New retirement homes target gays nearing 65. *The Seattle Times,* December 05, 1999.

A discussion of building "gay-friendly" retirement communities is presented, as a way to continue living in communities like those in which younger gays and lesbians live. How will these retirement communities differ from other retirement communities, and what is the purpose of building retirement communities that are marketed toward people of a specific sexual orientation?

Scholarly

1. Ehrenfeld, M., Bronner, G., Tabak, N., Alpert, R., Bergman, R. Sexuality among institutionalized elderly patients with dementia. *Nursing Ethics* Mar 1999, *6,* No. 2, p. 144 (*AN 1776142*).

The authors examined sexuality in elderly patients with dementia. Describe the structure of the study, including a brief discussion of the conclusions. What practical applications might come of this study?

Research Navigator Guide: Social Gerontology

2. Phanjoo, A. Sex and intimacy in older people. *Sexual & Relationship Therapy,* Aug 2002, *17,* No. 3, p. 229 (*AN 7175445*).

This editorial discusses articles regarding the effect of ageism on sexuality and intimacy, in an issue of the journal *Sexual and Relationship Therapy.* What concerns are raised regarding ageist stereotyping, and how do these stereotypes affect perceptions of sexuality in residents of long-term care facilities?

3. Walker, B., Harrington, D., Effects of staff training on staff knowledge and attitudes about sexuality. Sep 2002, *28,* No. 8, p. 639, (*AN 7317009*).

Sexuality in residents of long-term care facilities and staff members' attitudes toward sexuality in older people are discussed. What is the design of the study used to evaluate staff knowledge and attitude? What changes can be made to improve staff attitudes toward the expression of sexuality in older people?

Applied Research Exercises

1. Interview at least five people who work in a long-term care facility serving older adults (e.g. nursing, assisted living, adult family homes), regarding their attitudes toward sexuality of older clients in such a setting. Try to interview staff who represent different professions (e.g. nurse, social worker, nurse aide). Ask them to described their reaction and possible behavior in response to the following hypothetical situation:

   A woman resident, age 75, meets a man, aged 80, who has recently moved into the facility. Both have moderately advanced Alzheimer's disease. The two spend many hours together, holding hands, visiting each other's room. One morning, the staff member finds the man engaging in sex with the woman in her room. How would this staff person respond? Are there differences by the respondent's gender and profession?

2. Design a training program for all types of staff (e.g. social workers, nurses, administrators, physical and occupational therapists) who work in long-term care facilities, focusing on sexuality in old age, and implications for long-term care settings. Describe briefly the following:
   • What basic issues in aging and sexuality would you include?
   • What issues regarding caregiving for frail elders would you discuss?
   • To what extent should staff have a role in encouraging, discouraging, or tolerating sexuality among their elder residents?
   • Are there topics you would cover for specific types of staff?

CHAPTER 8

Social Theories of Aging

Feminism in Gerontology

Suggested Reading

Popular

1. Friedan, B. Why we marched, my darlings. *Time Magazine,* June 14, 1999.

Betty Friedan discusses her experiences as an early feminist. What is her commentary on women today and the progression of feminism from the 1960s? What significance does this commentary have for older women today?

2. Gomez, E. Power and glory in sisterhood. *New York Times,* October 13, 2002.

"Gloria: Another Look at Feminist Art in the 1970's", a show about early feminist art, is discussed in this article. Who were some leaders in early feminist thought and what were their ideas? Why is it important to revisit these ideas?

3. Schultz, C. Historian's simple quote inspires women. *The Seattle Times,* May 18, 2003.

This article discusses Laurel Thatcher Ulrich's famous quotation, "Well-behaved women rarely make history", as a means of comparing women of the 1970s and young women today. What inspired this quotation and what does it tell us about feminism of the 1960s and 1970s versus current feminist perspectives?

Scholarly

1. Cohen, H. Developing media literacy skills to challenge television's portrayal of older women. *Educational Gerontology,* 2002, *28,* No. 7, p. 599 (*AN 7253190*).

This article discusses the "double oppression" that older women face, as they are devalued for being old and also for being women. This study examined the role of television in reinforcing these images of older women, focusing on two episodes of *The Golden Girls.* Discuss the practical implications of this study for educators and gerontologists.

2. Roberts, C. 'Successful aging' with hormone replacement therapy: It may be sexist, but what if it works? *Science as Culture,* 2002, *11,* No. 1, p. 39 (*AN 6222478*).

Hormone replacement therapy and successful aging in women are discussed in this article. The author presents some individual women's experiences with HRT, as well as feminist responses to HRT. Briefly discuss the central feminist issues surrounding HRT.

3. Teubal, R. Women and elderly women in the mass media: Some preliminary notes. *Ageing International,* 2000, *25,* No. 4, p. 101 (*AN 4773901*).

This article discusses the impact of globalization and media portrayal of older women in Latin America. Pick one media image that the author presents and discuss its effect on perceptions of older women.

Applied Research Exercises

1. Conduct an informal survey with at least 10 women who are ages 50 and older, **and** who attended college between 1968 and 1978. Ask each woman to describe her experiences as a woman student in college during that era and the messages she heard, and how they may have affected her decisions regarding her career and family plans. To what extent have these women maintained the lifestyles they adopted during the height of the feminist movement? If they do not see themselves being affected by the events of that era, explore with each respondent why they were unaffected.

2. Consider the social demands on women who came of age in the 1930s, 1950s, and 1970s. As each of these cohorts of women have entered old age and advanced old age, to what extent can feminist theories explain their lives in their 60s, 70s and beyond?

New Developments in Social Theory

Suggested Reading

Popular

1. Duenwald, M. Power of positive thinking extends, it seems, to aging. *New York Times,* November 19, 2002.

The author discusses the relationship between happiness and long life. According to the article, what kind of optimism might be healthy, and when might pessimism play an important role longevity?

2. Nagourney, E. Social whirl may help keep the mind dancing. *New York Times,* October 29, 2002.

Research is reported that suggests that social contact is important to keeping the mind active and alert as we age. What elements of social contact appear to keep an individual's mind sharp? What does the author present as possible shortcomings of this study?

3. Ross, C., Mirowsky, J. Family relationships, social support and subjective life expectancy. *Journal of Health & Social Behavior,* 2002, *43,* No. 4, p. 469 (*AN 9382873*).

This article presents a new theory of mortality, which maintains that mortality is determined by a combination of how much reproductive life (i.e. years of continued ability to reproduce) remains, and the transfer effect, where parents live to invest in their children. This theory differs from the classic explanation of mortality, which focuses on natural selection and fertility at different points in life. What three problems with the classic theory of mortality are described in this paper?

Scholarly

1. Cutchin, M. P. The process of mediated aging-in-place: a theoretically and empirically based model, *Social Science & Medicine,* Sep 2003, *57,* No. 6, p. 1077 (*AN 10366479*).

This article examines the benefits of adult day centers and assisted living residences as two services that are based on the concept of aging-in-place.

Describe the theoretical model of "place integration" discussed in this article. What are the three core processes of place integration?

2. Putnam, M. Linking aging theory and disability models: Increasing the potential to explore aging with physical impairment. *The Gerontologist,* Dec 2002, *42,* No. 6, p. 799 (*AN 8736544*).

This article presents several social theories of aging that relate to aging with disability. Briefly summarize the different social theories presented in this article. According to this article, what are some reasons that social models of disability are important to gerontology?

3. Uhlenberg, P. Introduction: Why study age integration? *The Gerontologist,* Jun 2000, *40,* No. 3, p. 261 (*AN 3255732*).

This article discusses one way to approach the study of age integration. How is age integration defined in this article? What kinds of interactions and social settings are identified as optimal for age integration?

Applied Research Exercises

1. What are some elements of the most widely accepted social theories of aging that are described in Chapter 8 and in the readings above? Is it possible to combine these elements and create an overall theory that links these elements and applies to the broadest array of older adults?

2. Design a social theory of aging with disabilities that can be derived from several of the social theories of general aging described in Chapter 8 and in the readings above. How would you test such a theory in the population of adults with disabilities?

Social Constructionist Perspective on Aging

Suggested Reading

Popular

1. Anthony, T. Retirees in rockets, not rocking chairs—Glenn typifies new era of vigorous elders. *The Seattle Times,* January 16, 1998.

This article discusses the changing experience of aging and highlights activities that older people now participate in that they have not done in the past, from running marathons to bearing children past the age of 50. Discuss implications of these changes in the lifestyles of today's older adults for future research on aging. Do these changes mean that research outcomes should also change? Why or why not?

2. Taylor, L. Aging in perspective: our idea of who is old, who is young changes as we do. *The Seattle Times,* October 6, 2003.

The author discusses how perceptions of age change as people get older, and how our chronological definitions of "old" increase as we age. Discuss this phenomenon as it relates to a social constructionist theoretical perspective on the study of aging.

3. Vann, K. Old Age? Father time is looking younger. *The Seattle Times,* February 24, 1998.

This article discusses how the Baby Boomers, who began turning 50 in 1996, have modified society's attitudes toward aging. Give specific examples of ways in which attitudes toward aging and old are changing. How might this article support or refute the notion that researchers' own realities influence the gathering and interpretation of data?

Scholarly

1. Jost, J., Kruglanski, A. The estrangement of social constructionism and experimental social psychology: History of the rift and prospects for reconciliation. *Personality & Social Psychology Review,* 2002, *6,* No. 3, p. 168 (*AN 6860585*).

The authors review the history of social constructionism and experimental social psychology as two similar subcultures of social psychology. Discuss the origins and developments in social constructionist thought as described in this article. Explain how it is similar or different from experimental social psychology.

2. Sanchez, L. What do social constructionists want? *Journal of Marriage & the Family,* Nov 2002, *64,* No. 4, p. 1051 (*AN 7717932*).

The impact of constructionist theory on the study of family sociology is discussed. What arguments does the author present in favor of social constructionists over objectivists? How would you apply the pros and cons of this argument in understanding social gerontological processes?

3. Schaller, M. Any theory can be useful, even if it gets on our nerves. *Personality & Social Psychology Review,* 2002, *6,* No. 3, p. 199 (*AN 6860581*).

The author presents ways in which social constructionist themes and attitudes are useful in understanding aging as well as ways in which they are constraining. What are the benefits and constraints of using social constructionist theory in social gerontology? Give specific examples that you can derive from this article.

Applied Research Exercises

1. List ways in which social constructionist theory has been useful in explaining phenomena in social gerontology and other fields such as family sociology. How does this theory strengthen our understanding of these phenomena in each of these areas? Are there alternative theories of social gerontology from Chapter 8 that could also be applied readily to other areas of social gerontology?

2. Social constructionists are critical of the concepts of successful and productive aging that are discussed in this text. What are the primary criticisms of the concepts of successful and productive aging? Based on your readings, what concepts about aging across the life span, such as active aging and resiliency, might address some of these criticisms?

CHAPTER 9

The Importance of Social Supports: Family, Friends, Neighbors, and Communities

Gains for Multiple Generations from Intergenerational Programs

Suggested Reading

Popular

1. Melendez, M. Mentoring can work, if it's done correctly. *The Seattle Times,* March 29, 2003.

This article describes a mentorship program where an older adult is paired with a disadvantaged middle school student. What does the article list as possible benefits of the program? Under what circumstances might this program be ineffective?

2. Stripling, S. Green Lake first-graders make a difference in lives of elderly. *The Seattle Times,* December 15, 2002.

The Grandpals program, which builds partnerships between residents of a long-term care facility and elementary school children, is described. Children learn about some elders' physical limitations as well as their wisdom, while participating older people gain companionship and support from the children. In what ways might young children benefit from the Grandpals program? Are there any ways in which this program's approach could be harmful to children's perceptions of old age?

3. Teicher, S. Drumming up understanding between the generations. *Christian Science Monitor,* June 5, 2001, *93,* No. 133, p. 14 (*AN 4530602*).

The activities of the Peace Drum Project and other intergenerational programs are described in this report. These programs encourage interaction between children and older people. How have these projects been beneficial for both children and older participants? Identify strengths and weaknesses of each of the different activities, and describe how they added to or detracted from the goals of these programs.

Scholarly

1. Bullock, J., Osborne, S. Seniors', volunteers', and families' perspectives of an intergenerational program in a rural community. *Educational Gerontology,* Apr/May 99, *25,* No. 3, p. 237 (*AN 1926628*).

The authors designed and implemented the Befrienders Program, an intergenerational project for rural homebound older adults who wanted assistance and companionship. This program brought young adults into older adults' homes to assist them with chores and interact with them. Identify three benefits that the older adults experienced as a result of this activity, as well as three benefits for participating young adults.

2. Gross, D. Intergenerational daycare and preschoolers' attitudes about aging. *Educational Gerontology,* Apr 2002, *28,* No. 4, p. 271 (*AN 6472464*).

The author reports the findings of a study assessing children's perceptions of the older adults in an intergenerational daycare program. The study was conducted in light of mixed evidence regarding whether or not intergenerational contact positively influences children's attitudes about images of older people. How did children rate older adults vs. younger adults? Give at least three factors that influenced children's reactions to images of older and younger persons.

3. Knapp, J., Stubblefield, P. Changing students' perceptions of aging: The impact of an intergenerational service learning course. *Educational Gerontology,* Oct 2000, *26,* No. 7, p. 611 (*AN 3889095*).

An intergenerational service learning course was conducted with ten people over the age of 55, as well as traditional-age students. Together, these students learned about the processes of aging, followed by an assessment of what they learned. What did researchers derive from this study about creating more realistic views of aging? What other intergenerational programs do the authors suggest?

Applied Research Exercises

1. After reading these articles describing several creative intergenerational activity programs, design a study that brings together young children (ages 3–10) with older adults with chronic health conditions who live in the community. Identify measurable outcomes, such as how many elders and children remain in the program after one year, changes in attitudes toward aging and older adults among children, and frequency of direct interaction between the two different generations. How would you design the study in order to maximize the success of your intervention? Discuss any limitations to this intervention.

2. Design a service learning program with the shared goal of improving the social or physical environment, such as supports for homeless families or cleaning up the environment. While the focus of the program is on bringing generations together to address a social problem, a secondary outcome should be to improve older adults' attitudes toward college-age students and students' attitudes toward aging and the older population. After identifying a problem of concern to both generations, design an intergenerational program to address this. What would characterize the interactions between elders and college age students? How would this problem-based approach differ from programs focused only on attitudinal change?

Legal and Service Issues Faced by Gay and Lesbian Families

Suggested Reading

Popular

1. Slade, D. Decriminalizing homosexuality. *World & I,* Oct 2003, *18,* No. 10, p. 54 (*AN 10928016*).

The author discusses issues involved in the 2003 U.S. Supreme Court case *Lawrence v Texas,* in which a Texas law sought to criminalize homosexual relations. The article describes some benefits of marriage for gay and lesbian couples. What are these benefits and how do they affect homosexual couples as they age?

2. Mansnerus, L. New Jersey to recognize gay couples. *New York Times,* January 9, 2004.

In 2004, the New Jersey legislature passed a law to allow same-sex marriages in that state. The measure allows domestic partners to make medical decisions about each other, and also requires health insurance companies to offer coverage to domestic partners. This law also applies to heterosexual unmarried couples over the age of 62. What are some potential flaws in this measure, both according to those who oppose it and those who favor same-sex marriage?

3. Newman, M. Survivor in gay union appeals denial of benefits to boy. *New York Times,* October 15, 2003.

Several legal issues that lesbian and gay couples face when raising children are discussed in this story. The lesbian couple featured in this article had a son when one of the women became pregnant through a sperm donor. The other woman died shortly after. The surviving partner is fighting for Social Security benefits for their son. What is the surviving woman's argument in favor of receiving benefits? What legal obstacles stand in the way of obtaining Social Security benefits for the child? Given the obstacles in getting survivors benefits, what might be the implications of Social Security for homosexual partners in old age?

Scholarly

1. Isn't this gay, dear? *Economist,* November 23, 2002, *365,* No. 8300, p. 30 (*AN 8557917*).

This article describes a unique retirement community in southwest Florida, designed for older gays and lesbians and argues that more such retirement communities are needed. Discuss why there is a need for more of these retirement options, and describe elements of the Palms of Manasota Retirement Community that help it to better serve the gay and lesbian community than more traditional communities.

2. Recent cases: Family law. *Harvard Law Review,* Apr 2000, *113,* No. 6, p. 1551 (*AN 3165418*).

Among the cases reviewed, this article discusses issues of visitation between a child and a lesbian de facto parent. What is the court's definition of "de facto parent"? What two principles does this article describe that restricted the court's ability to intervene in the relationship between the parent and child in this situation? Can you think of any implications of these principles for child-lesbian parent relationships in old age?

3. Lin, T. Social norms and judicial decision-making: Examining the role of narratives in same-sex adoption cases. *Columbia Law Review,* Apr 1999, *99,* No. 3, p. 739 (*AN 2202752*).

This author makes the argument that social narratives influence the way decisions are made in adoption cases for same-sex partners, asserting that courts are biased against gays and lesbians. What does the author mean by "social narratives", and what is his basis for making the claims that courts are biased against gays and lesbians? Can you think of similar biases against gay and lesbian elders?

Applied Research Exercises

1. States, counties and cities have widely varying laws regarding the legal rights of gay and lesbian couples, and only nine states recognize same-sex domestic partnerships among public employees and their partners. They also vary in terms of laws prohibiting discrimination in housing, public employment and public accommodations. Your research project is to determine what the laws are in your city and state regarding the following:

    a. Prohibiting discrimination in public employment. In private employment.

    b. Prohibiting discrimination in housing and public accommodations, such as long-term care facilities

    c. Providing domestic partnership benefits. If so, identify the type, such as health benefits, dental benefits, bereavement/sick leave, registration of same-sex couples.

    d. If your state/city provides domestic partnership benefits, how does this differ from the legal rights bestowed by marriage?

    Summarize your findings by reflecting on the legal barriers that gays and lesbians face across the life span.

2. Communities differ widely in the social and support services available to older gays and lesbians. Try to identify the following in your community:

    a. Any services specifically for older gays and lesbians, such as a chapter of Senior Action in a Gay Environment (SAGE)

    b. Supports and services for caregivers of older adults

    c. Supports through religious institutions

    d. Supports through senior centers

    In locating such supports, you may need to call some agencies directly, such as the Area Agency on Aging, the information and referral line or a senior center to ask what kinds of services/supports they would provide for gay and lesbian elders.

Blended Families and Cross-Generational Relationships

Suggested Reading

Popular

1. Hayden, L. Have a 'sblended' holiday season. *Brown University Child & Adolescent Behavior Letter,* Nov 2000, *16,* No. 11, p. 5 (*AN 3717119*).

This article examines the challenges that different types of blended families face during the holiday season. What types of blended families are presented in this article? List at least three specific reasons why blended families often face family crises or tensions during the holiday season.

2. Faull, J. Do's and don'ts for stepparents. *The Seattle Times,* September 14, 2002.

In honor of National Stepfamily Day, the author offers suggestions to adults entering into stepfamilies. Select at least two suggestions from the list of "do's" and two from the list of "don'ts" that you think are most important for stepfamilies. Then discuss why they are important.

3. King, M. Grandparents vs. parents: 2 generations, 2 views of rights. *The Seattle Times,* October 18, 1999.

This article describes one blended family's approach to unifying their new family, and the problems that arise in determining the rights of paternal grandparents to visit their grandchildren after the father has died. What key question regarding grandparent rights was the U.S. Supreme Court trying to answer in this case? Describe and critique this blended family's approach to creating success in their new situation.

Scholarly

1. Myers, J., Schwiebert, V., Grandparents and stepgrandparents: Challenges in counseling the extended-blended family. *Adultspan: Theory Research & Practice,* Spring 1999, *1,* No. 1, p. 50 (*AN 5437485*).

The focus of this article is on counseling extended-blended families, emphasizing the grandparent-grandchild relationship. What stages are involved in adjusting to the role of a step-grandparent? What recommendations are made regarding maintaining harmony in the extended-blended family structure?

2. Stein, H., Brier, M. Yours, mine, and hours. *Financial Planning,* Mar 2002, *32,* No. 3, p. 61 (*AN 7273402*).

This article focuses on the financial challenges of blended families, emphasizing that it is necessary for the financial planner to understand the relations among each family member. Identify three suggestions that these authors give for financial planning in blended families.

3. The changing role of grandparents. *Christian Science Monitor,* September 5, 2001, *93,* No. 197, p. 14 (*AN 5105504*).

Findings of research on the changing role of grandparents due to divorce and other factors are discussed. Describe the research that was conducted and what it shows about the ways in which the role of grandparents changes following the divorce of parents.

Research Navigator Guide: Social Gerontology

Applied Research Exercises

1. AARP, the Child Welfare League and Generations United all have information on their websites regarding legal issues faced by grandparents when their adult children divorce and by step grandparents. Review these and at least two other websites (identified through links on these sites) to summarize

  a. the major legal issues faced by grandparents/step grandparents in instances of divorce/blended families

  b. current state legislation to protect grandparents' rights

  c. contemporary challenges to grandparents' legal rights by adult children

  Given what you have learned from these websites, clarify and summarize your own position/values related to grandparents rights vs. the rights of the parents.

2. Identify at least two blended families in your community. Interview at least two members from each family, preferably in a different age range. Ask them the following questions:

  a. What is the composition of their blended family?

  b. What are some of the greatest challenges for their blended family in coming together?

  c. How did they address those challenges?

  d. Recommendations that they would have for others who are forming blended families.

  Summarize and analyze these results in a way that would be useful for a social worker or psychologist who counsels blended or stepfamilies.

Research Navigator Guide: Social Gerontology

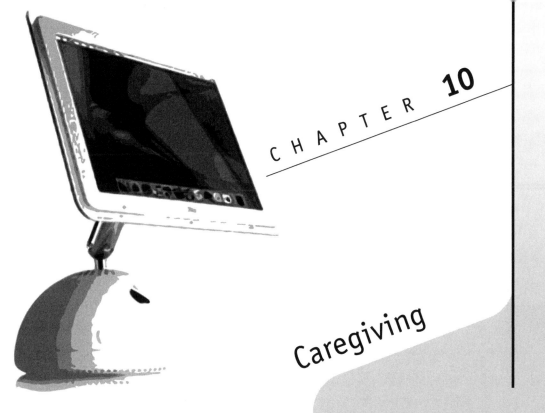

Caregiving

Elder Abuse

Suggested Reading

Popular

1. Pear, R. Unreported abuse found at nursing homes. *New York Times,* March 3, 2002.

The author highlights a recent report by The General Accounting Office on elder abuse. The study found that "alleged physical and sexual abuse of nursing home residents is frequently not reported in a timely manner," and that "few allegations of abuse are ultimately prosecuted." Cite three articles in *Content Select* that address the issue of unreported elder abuse in long-term care.

2. Discuss in depth the Elder Justice Act of 2003, H. R. 2490, introduced by Rep. Raum Emanuel. Discuss the bill's purpose and provisions. See website: http://www.elder-abuse-information.com/news/news_071103_hr2490.htm

3. The first National Elder Abuse Incidence Study states that adult children comprise the largest category of perpetrators of elder abuse.

Briefly discuss the varieties of elder maltreatment, i.e., physical, emotional, psychological etc. Identify at least three steps that are being taken to prevent mistreatment of older persons. See website: http://www.aoa.gov/eldfam/Elder_Rights/Elder_Abuse/AbuseReport_Full.pdf and http://www2.webmagic.com/abuse.com/index6.html

Scholarly

1. Anetzberger, G., Palmisano, B. A model intervention for elder abuse dementia. *The Gerontologist,* 2000, *40,* No. 4 (*AN 3639597*).

The authors describe a collaborative project that improved the management of elder abuse situations. They provide examples of education curriculum modules, cross training programs and handbooks for caregivers used in this project. Find at least two other projects that have been successful in preventing elder abuse.

2. Loue, S. Elder abuse and neglect in medicine and law: The need for reform. *Journal of Legal Medicine,* 2001, *22,* No. 2 (*AN 5356503*).

This article examines forms of elder abuse and neglect, and their implications for medicine and law in the U.S. Discuss legal standards in screening for elder abuse and differences in state laws on elder abuse.

3. Wolf, R. Suspected abuse in an elderly patient. *American Family Physician,* 1999, *59,* No. 5 (*AN 1674093*).

The author presents a case study of a typical elder-abuse situation and the challenges that health care professionals face when trying to resolve it. Find at least three more articles in *Content Select* that focus on cases of elder abuse; include action being taken to detect and prevent situations of elder abuse.

Applied Research Exercises

1. The *National Center on Elder Abuse* writes: "There is no federal law on elder abuse. The federal Older Americans Act (42 U.S.C. 3001 et seq., as amended) does provide definitions of elder abuse and authorizes the use of federal funds for the National Center on Elder Abuse and for certain elder abuse awareness, training, and coordination activities in states and local communities, but does not fund adult protective services or shelters for abused older persons." Discuss what legislation is being enacted in your own state to protect vulnerable seniors, including adult protective services for elders in the community and the long-term care ombudsman programs for institutional abuse.
2. Assume that you have the resources to design a family intervention program where gerontologists, social workers, psychologists, and

Research Navigator Guide: Social Gerontology

other experts could work together with older adults who are at risk for abuse. Discuss which members of the family should and should not be involved in such an intervention program. What is the rationale for your recommendations?

Gender Differences in Caregiving

Suggested Readings

Popular

1. Jackson, M. More sons are juggling jobs and care for parents. *New York Times,* June 15, 2003.

A new study has shown that more men are taking on the role of caregiver to elderly parents. Discuss the theory of "hidden caregiver" as described in the article.

2. Velkoff, V. A., Lawson, V. A. Gender and Aging. *International Brief: U.S. Bureau of the Census, U.S. Department of Commerce,* 1998.

The authors examine gender differences in caregiving among older adults—both as recipients and as givers of care. Discuss topics raised in the profile with respect to caregiving, such as an aging population, sandwich generation, older women living alone, institutionalization, and the importance of grandparents. Include at least two international studies referenced at the end of the report.

3. Jackson, M. Companies adding benefits for care of the elderly. *New York Times,* July 7, 2002.

For employers, geriatric care benefits make increasing sense. Corporate America loses around $11 billion a year because of absenteeism, turnover and lost productivity among full-time employees who care for their older family members, according to a 1997 study by the MetLife Mature Market Institute and the National Alliance for Caregiving. In what ways are employer-paid elder care benefits more cost-effective for businesses? What other, non-financial benefits does such an approach offer?

Scholarly

1. Bookwala, J. Schulz, R. A comparison of primary stressors, secondary stressors, and Depressive symptoms between elderly caregiving husbands and wives: The caregiver health effects study. *Psychology & Aging,* 2000, *15,* No. 4 (*AN 3907809*).

This article reviews some of the key findings of a major study of the health impact of older adults who are caring for a frail spouse. Describe some of the key differences between men and women who are spousal caregivers in terms of health outcomes.

2. Katz, S. J., Kabeto, M., Langa, K. M. Gender disparities in the receipt of home care for elderly people with a disability in the United States. *Journal of the American Medical Association,* 2000, *284,* No. 23, p. 3022–3027 (*AN3883860*).

This article addresses gender differences in receiving informal and formal home care, and its impact on family members' physical and psychological health. Discuss the design and outcome measures of the study and explain the conclusion that there are large gender disparities in home care of older persons.

3. Neufeld, A. Harrison, M. J. Unfulfilled expectations and negative interactions: nonsupport in the relationships of women caregivers. *Journal of Advanced Nursing,* 2003, *41,* No. 4 (*AN9079428*).

The purpose of this study was to describe women's experiences as caregivers for an adult relative with dementia. Identify the types of nonsupport discussed in this article, describe the research methods, findings and conclusions of this study.

Applied Research Exercises

1. The United Nations Development for Social Policy and Development, Programme on Ageing, UN Division for the Advancement of Women, International Institute on Aging issued "Caregiving and Older Person— Gender Dimensions" on their website: http://www.un.org/documents/ecosoc/cn6/1998/gendcare/cop97.htm
In the *Summary of the General Debate,* #10 states:

"Within the older population age 60 and above, older persons aged 80 and over are the fastest growing group in the world, with women generally surviving to older ages than men. Indeed, among people over age 75, almost two-thirds are women. Considering that persons in the age 80 and older group may be most often in need of support and care, the rapid increase in the world's very old obviously has implications for policies intended to assist family caregivers, the majority of whom are also women."

Design a caregiving model for women over 75 years old who are not disabled but have multiple chronic diseases. In what ways would your model address cultural differences in caregiving attitudes?

2. Interview at least three women and three men, ages 25–45, about their current activities in caregiving and their expectations regarding care-

giving of a parent, other relative or close friend in the future. What is the relationship between these adults' ages, gender, and current caregiving experience and their future caregiving expectations?

Grandparents as Caregivers

Suggested Reading

Popular

1. The elderly as caregivers. *Futurist,* Nov 1999, *33,* No. 9, p. 13 (*AN 2405669*).

Reports on the increasing number of older people who act as caregivers are given. According to the article, what has led to this increase? What comments does the author make about the institutionalization of caregiving in the United States?

2. Gardner, M. Creating new roles for grandparents. *Christian Science Monitor,* September 8, 1999, *91,* No. 198, p. 15 (*AN 2234854*).

The author discusses the celebration of Grandparents Day, recognizing the way the role of grandparents changed during the 1990s. What specific changes in the role of grandparents does the author identify? How do these changes affect their role as caregivers for grandchildren?

3. Holstrom, D. Grandfamilies: when parenting skips a generation. *Christian Science Monitor,* January 20, 1999, *91,* No. 37, p. 13 (*AN 1454301*).

According to this article, there is a lack of services for low-income grandparents who are raising their grandchildren. The author highlights a model program, entitled "GrandFamilies", which helps families with housing and social needs. What reasons does the author give for why more grandparents today are the primary guardians of their grandchildren? What kinds of services are needed most by these newly emerging families?

Scholarly

1. Blackstone, T. On being a grandmother. *Ageing International,* Winter 2000/Spring 2000, *26,* No. 3/4, p. 43 (*AN 5404865*).

This author discusses the changing role of grandparents, focusing on grandmothers in particular. What observations does the author make regarding the connection between employment for women and the role of grandmothers?

2. Ross, M. Reflections on grandparenthood. *Psychodynamic Practice,* May 2002, *8,* No. 2, p. 236 (*AN 7195618*).

Using a psychodynamic perspective, this article reflects on the meanings of being a grandparent. The author calls for a redistribution of family roles. What does the author advocate regarding such changes, and what other kinds of changes in the role of grandparents does she recommend?

3. Pizzey, E. Calling all grandparents. *Ageing International,* Winter/Spring 2000, *26,* No. 3/4, p. 13 (*AN 5404844*).

This article gives a description of the roles and responsibilities of grandparents in caring for their grandchildren, focusing on the way certain behaviors are passed down from grandparents to grandchildren. What does the author say about this phenomenon, and how might it change if the grandparent becomes the primary caregiver for young children?

Applied Research Exercises

1. Interview at least five people aged 20–40 from diverse ethnic groups who were raised by one or more of their grandparents or whose grandparents had a significant role in their upbringing. Interview another group of five people in the same age and ethnic groups who had a more distant relationship with all their grandparents, where no caregiving was involved. Ask each respondent to describe:
   a. How many grandparents they had while growing up, and which of these elders were involved in their upbringing. For those who did not have actively involved grandparents, what was the nature of their interactions?
   b. What are their earliest recollections of their grandparents who did and did not provide caregiving to them as they were growing up.
   c. As they were growing up, how often did they see each grandparent, including the grandparent(s) involved in their upbringing?
   d. What do they believe to be their responsibilities to their grandparents if the older person becomes frail and needs some assistance?
   e. What adjectives would they use to describe "old age" and "older people?"

   To what extent do the responses of these two groups of young adults reflect the nature of their childhood experiences with grandparents? Are there differences between those who did and did not receive caregiving from their grandparents? Are there ethnic differences within each group, or are the ethnic differences that emerge reflective of the respondents' childhood experiences with grandparents?
2. Based on the readings above and in Chapter 10, make a list of the advantages and disadvantages of children being raised by their grandparents. Compare that with a similar list of advantages and disadvantages of children observing their parents caring for grandparents.

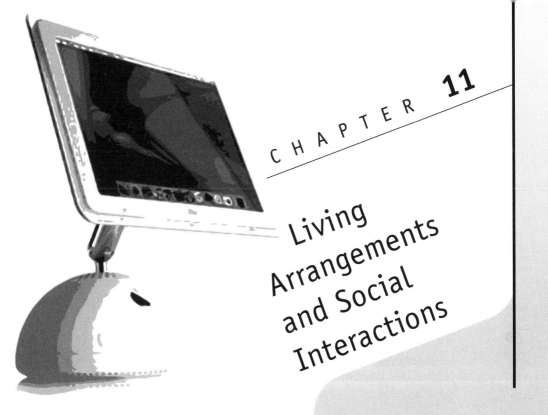

CHAPTER **11**

Living Arrangements and Social Interactions

Underpaid Staff in Long-Term Care Facilities

Suggested Reading

Popular

1. The Wellspring Model, website http://www.wellspring.ca/innovation/?parent=23, was developed by a team of oncology experts, working closely with cancer patients, family members, and caregivers. The model seeks to give direct care staff greater say in decision-making about quality of care and the nature of their jobs. It has resulted in lower staff turnover, more staff vigilance in assessing patient problems, and better quality of life for residents, with no additional costs to the facility. Discuss at least three key features that focus on making the nursing home a better place to live by improving clinical care and making it a better place to work by giving employees the skills they need and a voice in how their work should be performed.

2. Hollinger-Smith, L. It takes a village to retain quality nursing staff. *Nursing Homes Long Term Care Management,* 2003, Vol 52 No 5. Website www.nursinghomesmagazine.com

The author examines the Mather Institute on Aging in Evanston, Il. This long-term care provider uses the 3 "Rs" of employee retention—relationships, respect, and recognition—to reduce the turnover of direct care staff. One outgrowth of this is the Illinois LEAP program—a comprehensive LTC workforce initiative that aims to educate, empower, and retain staff. Identify and discuss its two modules on how to work with diverse staff in nursing homes.

3. Fagan, R. M. Turning the tables. *Assisted Living Today,* Vol 9, No 8 www.alfa.org

Examples are given of assisted living communities that have incorporated culture change models into their system of care and have experienced a decrease in staff turnover, reduction in resident medication use and the elimination of temporary staff. In what ways would you expect such a culture change model to reduce problems with turnover in other types of long-term care?

Scholarly

1. Harrington, C, Kovner, C. Experts recommend minimum nurse staffing standards for nursing facilities in the United States. *The Gerontologist,* 2000, No. 40, p. 5–16 *(AN3004316).*

The authors discuss a conference that focused on the issue of nurse staffing and quality care in nursing facilities. Identify at least three recommendations made by the panel of experts to improve quality of nursing home care for frail elders.

2. McDonald, C. Recruitment, retention and recognition of frontline workers in long-term care. *Generations,* 2003, *23* No. 3, p. 41–42.

The author examines how the Geriatric Nursing Assistance Specialist (GNAS) program allows certified nursing assistants (CNAs), after successfully completing the program, to assume an expanded and/or leadership role within a facility. Identify the three key elements to the program. Discuss how this program increases self-esteem in the CNA plus enhances quality of care for the residents in long-term care facilities.

3. Feldman, P. H. Work life improvements for home care workers: impact and feasibility. *The Gerontologist,* 1993, Vol 33, p. 47–54.

This article details the results of four demonstration projects designed to upgrade home aide employment, reduce turnover, and increase continuity of care. Based on your understanding of caregiving, what factors would you expect could improve the work life of staff and, in turn, the quality of care provided by paid caregivers?

Research Navigator Guide: Social Gerontology

Applied Research Exercises

1. Stone, R. and Weiner, J. co-authored the book, *Who will care for us? Addressing the long-term care workforce crisis.* The publisher's website http://www.urban.org/RobynIStone gives the following synopsis of the book:

"The paraprofessional long-term care workforce—nursing assistants, home health and home care aides, personal care workers, and personal care attendants—forms the centerpiece of the formal long-term care system. These front-line workers provide hands-on care, supervision, and emotional support to millions of elderly and younger people with chronic illness and disabilities. Low wages and benefits, hard working conditions, heavy workloads, and a job that has been stigmatized by society make worker recruitment and retention difficult."

Given the current reality of low wages and benefits in long-term care, together with high employment rates, design a program to recruit, train and motivate employees for nursing homes and home health care.

2. Discuss what factors may influence an organization's success in recruiting and retaining experienced staff caregivers. For some ideas on what researchers have found, see: Wellman, J. Simple truths about staff retention" *Provider* 2002, *28,* Full text of article can be found in: www.providermagazine.com/pdf/human-09–2002.pdf.

New Options in Long-Term Care

Suggested Reading

Popular

1. Brenner, E. Making a residence for the elderly more like home. *New York Times,* May 5, 2002.

New options are emerging in adult care facilities for older persons who are able to live relatively independent lives and are in good health. What new types of facilities are available now for older adults, according to this article?

2. King, M. Providers fighting assisted-living rules that would raise standards. *The Seattle Times,* September 8, 2003.

This article discusses the reaction of operators of assisted living facilities to efforts by the state of Washington to raise standards for residents. How are regulations for assisted-living facilities different from those for other long-term care facilities, and what effect does this difference have on the type of care available to frail older persons?

3. Taylor, L. What to ask to help determine level of assistance a facility offers. *The Seattle Times,* January 12, 2004.

The author describes various options in long-term care to suit the needs of different individuals. What different kinds of facilities are discussed, and what types of older adults do they serve? According to the author, what are some important issues that older persons and their families should consider when selecting a long-term care facility?

Scholarly

1. Kemper, P. Long-term care research and policy. *Gerontologist,* Aug 2003, *43,* No. 4, p. 436 (*AN 10870396*).

This article discusses the contributions of long-term care research to policy. What new developments in long-term care research are discussed in this article, and what policy issues regarding long-term care are most in need of research?

2. Phillips, C., Munoz, Y., Sherman, M., Rose, M., Spector, W., Hawes, C. Effects of facility characteristics on departures from assisted living: Results from a national study. *Gerontologist,* Oct 2003, *43,* No. 5, p. 690 (*AN 11452524*).

The authors studied characteristics of assisted living facilities that affected whether or not residents chose to remain in them. What factors influenced older persons in their decisions to leave assisted living facilities, and what impact does this information have on the future design of long-term care facilities?

3. Stevens, L. Glass, R. Nursing homes. *Journal of the American Medical Association,* 2001, *286,* No. 19, p. 2498 (*AN 5533373*).

A brief overview of the changing nature and clientele of nursing homes is presented. How are the characteristics and services of nursing homes defined? How should an older person go about choosing a nursing home, according to this article?

Applied Research Exercises

1. Make a list of the characteristics of an "ideal" nursing home and an "ideal" assisted living facility. In this case, "ideal" is the type of facility where you would want to live, or where you would choose to have an older relative live if they needed long-term care. Are there differences in the features, policies, and activities of each type of facility?

2. Interview at least five adults who have parents aged 75 and older regarding their preferences for long-term care options for their parents.

Research Navigator Guide: Social Gerontology

Ask each person if they have considered what would be best for their parents, and if they have discussed these options with their parents. To what extent do the adult children and their parents agree regarding the best type of long-term care for them? To what extent are these residential vs. community-based long-term care options?

Retirement Relocation

Suggested Reading

Popular

1. Brock, F. How much will you need to retire? It helps to plan. *New York Times,* March 17, 2002.

In this article, the author focuses on the effect of financial planning on retirement. The author suggests that many people are mistaken about the cost of retirement, and that relocating may make retirement more affordable. Which cities does he list as most affordable, and what resources are available to help older adults plan for their retirement?

2. Housing selection crucial for retirees. USA Today Magazine, 2003, *132* No. 2700, p. 8 (*AN 10818606*).

This article provides advice for retirees on selecting housing options. Based on this article, discuss the different factors that retirees should consider when deciding where to live upon retirement.

3. Perry, J. For most, there's no place like home. *U.S. News & World Report,* June 4, 2001, *130,* No. 22 (*AN4487248*).

The article focuses on how the in-migration of large numbers of retirees affects communities. The author cites examples of some cities' efforts to improve services for the growth of their older population. Select three cities described in this article where many seniors have retired and discuss how the communities have changed.

Scholarly

1. Castle, N. G., "Relocation of the elderly," *Medical Care Research & Review,* 2001, *58* No. 3, p. 291 (*AN 6389566*).

How does the author define "relocation?" According to this article, what kinds of social and psychological changes do relocated elders most often experience?

2. Koenig, C. S., Cunningham, W. R. Adulthood relocation: Implications for personality, future orientation, and social partner choices. *Experimental Aging Research,* 2001, *27,* No. 2 *(AN 4275189).*

This article discusses relocation in adulthood by comparing the process in different age groups. What are the three types of moves for later life adults that are presented in the article? What does this article suggest about why some individuals are more likely to relocate than others?

3. Sugihara, S., Evans, G. W. Place attachment and social support at continuing care retirement communities. *Environment & Behavior,* 2000, *32,* No. 3, p. 400 *(AN 3075319).*

Relocation to retirement communities is discussed in terms of social support and place attachment. According to this article, what role do physical features of the environment play in retirement communities to encourage social support and attachment to place?

Applied Research Exercises

1. Conduct an informal survey of your friends and relatives ages 40 and older. Ask them if they have thought of relocation to another community, state or country after they retire. Ask them to list what would motivate them to relocate, and what they would want in the place where they decide to relocate. Then compare these open-ended responses to the list of reasons for retirement relocation listed in the articles above and in Chapter 11. To what extent is your informal respondent group representative of the larger samples studied in these publications?
2. Design a retirement relocation checklist that older adults who are contemplating relocating could use to decide if they should or should not retire, the type of housing and living styles they would want, and what elements are most important to them in determining when and where to retire.

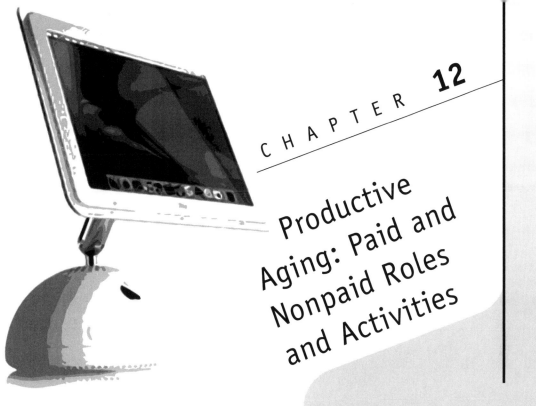

CHAPTER 12

Productive
Aging: Paid and
Nonpaid Roles
and Activities

Poverty in Old Age

Suggested Reading

Popular

1. Armas, G. More Americans are postponing retirement, working past 65. *The Seattle Times,* May 21, 2003.

A growing number of people are working past age 65, due primarily to economic concerns as well as better health among today's cohort of older people. Give three examples of specific economic and health reasons why this increase may be occurring.

2. Kleinfield, N. R. Golden years, on $678 a month. *New York Times,* September 3, 2003.

This article describes the struggles of a 68-year-old woman, who is living in poverty in New York City, where the problem of poverty in older people is worse than in other parts of the country. What factors contribute to this woman's poverty as she gets older, even though she was not poor when she was younger? What factors would explain the higher poverty rate in New York City?

3. Rosenbaum, D. Bush signs law to cover drugs for the elderly. *New York Times,* December 9, 2003.

The author discusses changes made by the new Medicare Prescription Drug law. What are the issues are raised regarding how these changes will affect older people who live in poverty in the United States?

Scholarly

1. McLaughlin, D., Jensen, L. Work history and U.S. elders' transitions into poverty. *Gerontologist,* Aug 2000, *40,* No. 4, p. 469 (*AN 3639593*).

This article describes a study on the relationship between employment history and older people's transition into poverty in the United States. How did the authors measure poverty? What risks do men and women face in becoming poor in late life, and how do the risks differ between men and women?

2. Van Hook, J. SSI eligibility and participation among elderly naturalized citizens and noncitizens. *Social Science Research,* Mar 2000, *29,* No. 1, p. 51 (*AN 2875895*).

Factors that determine welfare eligibility across all age groups in the United States are studied. What are these factors, and to what extent are older adults dependent on welfare, as defined by SSI and Medicaid?

3. Vartanian, T., McNamara, J. Older women in poverty: The impact of midlife factors. *Journal of Marriage & the Family,* May 2002, *64,* No. 2, p. 532 (*AN 6569767*).

This study examines midlife and late-life factors that contribute to more older women living in poverty than their male counterparts. List three midlife and three late-life factors described in this article that may affect poverty levels in older women. Why is it important to study poverty in older women? How can late-life events influence poverty in older women, even if midlife characteristics contribute to economic well-being?

Applied Research Exercises

1. Your objective is to determine how well the current cohort of retired elders has prepared for their economic security during retirement. Interview at least five men and five women who have been retired for three or more years. Ask each one:
   a. How old were they when they retired?
   b. What were the primary reasons for their retirement?
   c. What type of work did they do before retiring?
   d. How many consecutive years did they work (full-time, part-time) before retiring?

e. Are they currently employed outside the home? (If yes, number of hours they work per week?)

f. What sources of income do they currently have (e.g. employment, pensions, Social Security, savings)?

g. Are they satisfied with their retirement economic status?

As you review the responses of each of these elders, do you see a pattern in their history of employment, their age at retirement and their sources of income? Among those who continue to work, is there any association between current and pre-retirement employment experiences?

2. Your objective is to determine if young and middle-aged people are preparing for financial security during their retirement. Interview at least five people age 20 to 30, and five age 40 to50. Be sure to have a mix of men and women. Ask each one:

a. At what age do they plan to retire?

b. Are they currently saving for retirement? More specifically:

- Do they have a retirement savings account through their work and for how long?
- Do they contribute to a workplace pension plan and for how long?
- Do they contribute to an independent retirement plan (e.g. IRA) and for how long?

c. Do they anticipate that they will receive Social Security when they retire? If not, why not?

As you review your findings, what are some differences by age, gender and types of retirement accounts?

Productive Aging

Suggested Reading

Popular

1. Finkel, D. Stuck behind the counter: Retirement is elusive dream for women. *The Seattle Times,* October 7, 2003.

The economic need for many women to continue working in old age is discussed in this article. How does the percentage of older women who are still employed compare to the percentage of older men working? What factors are contributing to the increase in older workers today?

2. McGeehan, P. Dealing with aging executives who just won't quit. *New York Times,* February 2, 2003.

This article discusses the conflict for people who choose to work past the age of 65, since most companies encourage their employees to retire before or by the age of 65. Pick one specific case presented in this article and discuss that person's motivation for working past the age of 65. How is "productivity" measured in this article?

3. Trafford, A. Retired but not resting: Older Americans turn to volunteering. *The Seattle Times,* January 6, 2003.

The author describes a changing trend in the growth in the number of people who volunteer after retirement. The article focuses on the contributions that retired people can make through volunteering to maintain a sense of their own productivity and to serve their communities. What physical and psychological health benefits are associated with volunteering during retirement?

Scholarly

1. Kumashiro, M. Ergonomic strategies and actions for achieving productive use of an ageing work-force. *Ergonomics,* Jul 2000, *43,* No. 7, p. 1007 (*AN 3387894*).

The author discusses the idea of using ergonomics in job settings in communities with low birth rates and an aging work force as a way to achieve productive aging. How does ergonomics serve to increase older workers' productivity? What does the author mean by the term, "productive aging" and how does it differ from the definition of this concept in Chapter 12? How does the author's definition of "productivity" affect the way success in aging is measured in general?

2. Ranzjin, R. The potential of older adults to enhance community quality of life: Links between positive psychology and productive aging. *Ageing International,* Winter 2003, *28,* No. 1, p. 30 (*AN 9405854*).

The aim of this article is to change attitudes toward older people, emphasizing the resources they can bring to society rather than viewing them as a burden. How does this article illustrate the way in which older people enhance quality of life for others in their communities? What practical implications are presented?

3. Weaver, J. Gerontology education: A new paradigm for the 21st century. *Educational Gerontology,* 1999, *25,* No. 6, p. 479 (*AN 2372115*).

This article seeks to dispel myths about the problems of aging and focuses on providing education about successful and productive aging. How does the author address the meaning of productive aging, and how does the article address aging as an issue of diversity?

Applied Research Exercises

1. Consider the definitions of "productive aging" as this concept is used in the articles listed above and in Chapter 12. Are there similarities across these articles and in your textbook? Do you see any biases in how productivity is defined? If so, does this reflect a Western cultural perspective or an employed person's bias toward this concept? Are there biases in terms of gender or ethnic minority status? List some characteristics that these definitions share and those that are unique to each of the readings above and in Chapter 12.

2. Interview at least 5 middle-aged and older adults who are retired and 5 who are still employed, with a mixture of men and women in each group. Ask each one to define the concept of "productive aging." Are there similarities between the definitions of these two groups of adults? Are there differences, and to what extent do these differences reflect the gender and/or the employment status of the respondent?

Religiosity/Spirituality

Suggested Reading

Popular

1. Associated Press. Religion is good for seniors' health, researchers find. *The Seattle Times,* August 11, 1998.

This article discusses a study that links religious practice to low blood pressure. The study found that among people who are over 65 years old, those who regularly participate in religious activities are 40 percent less likely to have high blood pressure. Why might religious activity affect a person's blood pressure? On the other hand, explain why it is important not to assume that religion *causes* good health.

2. Fuchs, M. New clerics seek ways to reach aging flocks. *New York Times,* August 9, 2003.

Relationships between young religious leaders and older members of religious communities are addressed. The author suggests that people are more likely to attend regular religious services as they age. In what ways might this trend affect the guidance provided to older adults by younger leaders in religious communities?

3. Religious struggle could prove fatal. *BBC News,* August 13, 2001. http://news.bbc.co.uk/1/hi/health/1488686.stm

According to a study reported in this article, older people with physical illnesses may actually experience a decline in their religious beliefs. The study showed that those who felt abandoned by God in sickness were more likely to die than those who still held strong religious beliefs. Does this mean that religion has a direct effect on health and survival? Why or why not?

Scholarly

1. Crowther, M., Parker, M., Achenbaum, W., Larimore, W., Koenig, H. Rowe and Kahn's model of successful aging revisited: Positive spirituality—the forgotten factor. *Gerontologist,* Oct 2002, *42,* No. 5, p. 613 (*AN 7453151*).

The authors discuss the importance of spirituality for the well-being of older adults. What distinctions do the authors make between religion, spirituality, and positive spirituality? How does each of these concepts appear to affect the health of older adults? Briefly describe Rowe and Kahn's model of successful aging, which is described in Chapter 6 and how positive spirituality may or may not be a relevant factor in the model.

2. Fry, P. Religious involvement, spirituality and personal meaning for life: Existential predictors of psychological well-being in community-residing and institutional care elders. *Aging & Mental Health,* Nov 2000, *4,* No. 4, p. 375 (*AN 4176430*).

This study examines the role of spirituality in the well-being of older people living in nursing homes and in the community. The researchers found a positive relationship between spirituality and well-being. What other factors may influence well-being in later life? Do they have a stronger or weaker effect than spirituality on well-being? What differences were found in this survey between institutionalized and community-dwelling older adults?

3. Parker, M., Bellis, J., Bishop, P., Harper, M., Allman, R., Moore, C., Thompson, P. A multidisciplinary model of health promotion incorporating spirituality into a successful aging intervention with African American and white elderly groups. *Gerontologist,* Jun 2002, *42,* No. 3, p. 406 (*AN 6815503*).

A health intervention with older people and their adult children is described, which tests the possibility of incorporating spirituality in a health promotion program with both whites and African Americans. Describe the health promotion model presented in this article. Discuss how spirituality was included in this study and whether it would be feasible to do so in a larger health promotion effort.

Applied Research Exercises

1. Based on the articles summarized above and the discussion of religiosity and spirituality among older adults in Chapter 12, make a list of the findings from the various studies that have examined these concepts. For each finding you list, specify if the researchers initially intended to study religiosity or spirituality, how they defined the concept, and what outcome variable(s) they used to test the impact of religiosity or spirituality (e.g. blood pressure, depression, recovery from surgery, health behaviors). Indicate if the results supported a link between the religiosity or spirituality and health outcomes.

2. Interview two young-old (age 65 to 75) and two oldest-old (over age 85) adults. Ask them about if they consider themselves to be a religious person. If they do, how do they define their religiosity? Has this changed over time? Do they make a distinction between being religious or spiritual? If so, how?

CHAPTER 13

Death, Dying, Bereavement, and Widowhood

Advance Directives

Suggested Reading

Popular

1. Roha, R, Esbenshade, A. Your WILL be done. *Kiplinger's Personal Finance* Jan 2004, *58,* No. 1, p. 80 (*AN 11644005*)

The authors explain the application of advance directives in estate planning. The first advance directive, a durable power of attorney for health care, appoints a person to be your health-care agent or proxy to make medical decisions for you if you can't do so yourself. The second, a living will, spells out the kinds of medical treatment you do and do not want if you are unable to speak for yourself. It generally applies only if a person is terminally ill and faces imminent death—or if he or she is in a persistent vegetative state. Advance directives should be tailored to your needs. Thus said, define your top five priorities for your own advance directive.

2. Chatzky, J. A will for the living. *Time* November 3, 2003 *162,* No. 18, p. 103 (*AN11195638*)

The author discusses the importance of writing a living will that references life support treatment. She cites the case of Terri Schiavo, a woman who was in a vegetative state for six years and had not put in her writing what her wishes would be regarding life supports; Chatzky emphasizes the importance of using a power of an attorney for health care and of naming a health care proxy. Why do you think people avoid writing a living will? Would you want to have life support? Explain why or why not.

3. Dulaney, E Going gently. *Indianapolis Monthly,* Nov 2003, *27* No. 3, p. 124, *(AN1187043)*

A Do Not Resuscitate order (DNR) is a request that no one attempt cardiopulmonary resuscitation if you quit breathing or your heart stops. This article examines various aspects of DNR. A DNR, like a living will or a durable power of attorney, is considered an "advance directive": a document that outlines your wishes about your medical care and other end-of-life issues in the event that you become too ill to make decisions for yourself. Anyone of sound mind can draw up a DNR, but people who have a terminal illness and no chance of recovery usually implement the orders. Do you want a DNR—why or why not? Even if the medical staff has agreed that there is no chance for recovery, would you want to be resuscitated?

Scholarly

1. Sypher, B. Initiating discussions about advance directives: the family physician's role. *American Family Physician* June 15, 2002, *65,* No. 12, p. 2443 *(AN 6870938)*.

The author writes an editorial on the role of the family physician in initiating advance directives, living wills or medical powers of attorney designed to clarify the patient's medical wishes. What are the advantages of initiating *advance* care planning discussions with patients when they are relatively healthy? What are the pros and cons of *advance* directives?

2. Scanlon, C. Ethical concerns in end-of-life care. *American Journal of Nursing* Jan 2003, *103* No. 1, p. 48, *(AN 9213289)*

The author reports on the ethical aspects of palliative care nursing in the United States and discusses various types of advance planning. Identify the key ethical issues in these types of advance planning.

3. Editors, *Cancer Weekly.* Oncology nurses need many things changed to best assist with advance directives *Cancer Weekly,* May 27, 2003, p. 94 *(AN 9850245)*

This editorial cites recent research that has found many problems in the process of completing and executing advance directives. Many issues remain to be studied. Describe why communication between the nurse and cancer patient on this subject is considered by the editors to be of vital importance.

Applied Research Exercises

1. Locate websites that include an example of a living will recognized by health care staff in your state. Complete this living will for yourself. Identify areas where you are uncertain regarding what actions you would like to be taken. Then discuss these areas with a close family member. Ask them if they would be comfortable making sure that your living will was implemented and adhered to if you were unable to make a decision about your end of life care. From your perspective, list any limitations of a living will.

2. Interview at least four members of your family or among your friends regarding their knowledge and attitudes toward advance directives and end of life care. Ask them the following questions:

   a. Do they know what advance directives are?

   b. Within the category of advance directives, do they know what a durable power of attorney is? A living will? A Do Not Resuscitate Order?

   c. Have they made any plans for end of life care for themselves if they were unconscious, comatose or mentally incompetent?

   d. If they have not specified end of life wishes in writing, what are the reasons that they have not done so?

   e. Have they ever had a discussion with their loved ones regarding end of life decisions? If not, what has prevented them from doing so?

   f. Based on this information, do you anticipate making changes with regard to planning for end of life care either for yourself or your loved ones?

Hospice

Suggested Reading

Popular

1. Painter, K. At core of care is the personal touch. *USA Today* Dec 30, 2003 *(ANJOE104773209903)*.

More than 50 percent of Americans who die of cancer and more than 25 percent who die of any cause now receive hospice care to ease pain and suffering in their final days, says the National Hospice and Palliative Care Organization. The organization, based in Alexandria, Va., estimates that about 20,000 nurses are involved in hospice care, most of which takes place in patients' homes. They are part of teams that include doctors, home health aides, social workers, chaplains and volunteers. What distinguishes hospice care from other types of end of life care?

2. Landro, L. Tough times for the spiritual side of healing. *Wall Street Journal* Dec. 18, 2003, *242,* No. 120 (*AN 11706443*).

The author focuses on the connection between spirituality and healing and how recent changes to medical laws may restrict a patient's access to spiritual services. Explain why spiritual care would be important to a dying patient, even though evidence of its impact is mixed. What arguments would you make for increasing Medicare funding for training chaplains to work with the terminally ill?

3. Berwick, C. Bono and the wolf. *Art News* Nov 2003 (*AN 11328290*).

The author reports on the work done by Irish rock star Bono for the benefit of the Irish **Hospice** Foundation. Bono's paintings illustrate the classic tale 'Peter and the Wolf'; what are other art forms that could be used to convey the work of Hospice and raise money for this type of organization?

Scholarly

1. Jacobs, S. Death by voluntary dehydration—what caregivers say. *New England Journal of Medicine,* July 24, 2003, *349,* No. 4, p. 325 (*AN 10315354*).

A survey found that nearly twice as many of the hospice nurse respondents had cared for patients who chose voluntary refusal of food and fluids to hasten death as had cared for patients who chose physician-assisted suicide. According to the author, the nurses' descriptions of the deaths resulting from voluntary refusal of food and fluids accord with published anecdotes that suggest it is a peaceful way to die. Cite three reasons why the author was hesitant to publish the data.

2. Staff. Whose life is it, anyway? Where family tragedy meets the separation of powers. *Economist;* 11/1/2003, *369,* No. 8348, (*AN 11269346*).

Terri Schiavo, who lies in a persistent vegetative state in a Florida hospice, has become the central figure in one of the most grievous medical, legal and family disputes of recent times. Mrs. Schiavo's case is about the medical state someone must be in before it becomes merciful to let them die. It is also about the family's agony when trying to decide what is right for those who cannot decide for themselves. What is the definition of death, as expressed by this article?

3. Joch, A. Final reunions. *Hospitals and Health Networks* Nov 2003, *77,* No. 11, p. 30, (*AN 11425261*).

The author reports on the hospice program in hospitals in Atlantic City, New Jersey. Most hospices care for families as well as patients, but not every program emphasizes outreach in broken relationships. Relief sometimes comes from soothing past emotional and psychological hurts that resurface when someone is dying. Is it important or not to mend a broken relationship if facing your own death? Why or why not?

4. Wood, T. Caring and comfort at the end of life. *Quest: Muscular Dystrophy Association* Nov/Dec 2003, *10,* No. 6, p. 42, (*AN 11421353*).

The author examines end-of-life care for patients with neuromuscular diseases and gives background on the concept of hospice. Explain why you think the team approach used in hospice care is important to the terminally ill patient and the family.

Applied Research Exercises

1. Identify the hospice programs in your community, which may be within hospitals, nursing homes or in the home of the dying person. Then interview at least three staff with different care responsibilities in one of these hospice programs. Ask them:
   a. What are the reasons that they have chosen to work in hospice care?
   b. What do they see as distinctive about hospice care?
   c. How does caring for the dying affect their own lives?
   d. What do they do to ensure that they do not get "burned out" from caring for the dying?
   e. Is there anything about hospice care that they would like to change?
   Based on your interviews, summarize what characteristics seem to distinguish hospice staff from other types of health care providers.
2. Imagine yourself as terminally ill. Based on what you have learned, design your own end of life plan. What would be important to you at the end of your life? How would you like to spend your last days if you were terminally ill? Where would you like to receive care—at home or in an institutional setting? Who would you want to be involved in your dying? Write down your end of life care plans and share them with a family member or loved one.

Physician Assisted Suicide

Suggested Reading

Popular

1. Fischer, MA. To Live or To Die *Reader's Digest* May 2003, *162,* No. 973: (*AN 9627085*)

The author focuses on the debate over the right of terminally ill patients to end their lives painlessly. Implications of an Oregon lawsuit related to the state's Death With Dignity Act are discussed along with arguments for and against physician-assisted suicide and the risks associated with the use of barbiturates. According to the article, what are some of the pressures experienced by terminally ill patients who choose to end their lives?

2. Lustig, A. End of Life Decisions *Commonweal* May 23, 2003, *130,* No. 10, p. 7, 1p (*AN 9902277*)

Several issues related to end-of-life decisions are discussed. These include the stages of dying, the role of physician-assisted suicide, and ethical and pastoral issues at the end of life. To what extent do these issues affect the way that terminally ill patients are cared for in the U.S?

3. Johnson, K. Judge upholds Oregon's assisted suicide law *USA Today* 4/18/02, p. A03 (*AN JOE06914385002*)

The article reports on a U.S. District Judge's ruling that Attorney General John Ashcroft could not nullify the Oregon Death with Dignity Act that allows physicians to help terminally ill patients kill themselves. Ashcroft issued a directive saying the prescription of lethal doses of medication served no "legitimate medical purpose" and ordered the Drug Enforcement Administration to terminate the prescription licenses of doctors who prescribed lethal doses, a move that would have nullified the Oregon law. What were the reasons that the District Judge rule against Ashcroft's directive. Do you think the Justice Department overstepped its authority?

Scholarly

1. Batlle, J. D. Legal Status of Physician-Assisted Suicide *Medical Student Journal of the American Medical Association (MSJAMA)* 5/7/2003, *289,* No. 17 p. 2279 (*AN 9688687*)

The author examines the gradual extension of legal rights in the end-of-life arena and argues that the physician-assisted suicide (PAS) debate has prompted a greater appreciation for improving palliative care, clarified patient wishes through advance directives, and brought patient self-determination to the forefront of end-of-life care. Can you identify other benefits for terminally ill patients that have resulted from the legal debates about physician-assisted suicide?

2. Akabayashi, A. Euthanasia, assisted suicide and cessation of life support: Japan's policy, law, and an analysis of whistle blowing in two recent mercy killing cases. *Social Science & Medicine* Aug. 2002, *55,* No. 4 p. 517 (*AN 8764760*).

The author examines two cases of mercy killings in Japan within the context of Japanese law. Compare how euthanasia and the cessation of life support are addressed in Japan and in the state of Oregon. To what extent are the laws in Japan similar or different from legal guidelines in Oregon's Death with Dignity Act?

3. Richardson, A. E. Death with dignity: the ultimate human right. *Humanist* July/Aug. 2002 *62,* No. 4 p. 42 (*AN 6858327*).

This essay explores the issue of death with dignity. The author argues that the morality of today's medical establishment has not evolved to take into account the quality of life for those who are dying. She suggests that a paradigm shift is needed in the educational curriculum of medical schools. Discuss what she means by a paradigm shift, and barriers to such major changes occurring.

Applied Research Exercises

1. Interview at least 10 men and women, ranging in age from 18 to 80, regarding their attitudes toward physician-assisted suicide. Ask each one what they would do if they had a terminal illness that made them bedridden and in constant pain, if physician assisted suicide were a legal option in their state/country. If they would want the option of physician-assisted suicide, how would they respond in finding a physician to assist them? In reviewing their responses, do you find differences by gender? By age? By ethnic minority status? Then ask a similar set of questions regarding their attitude toward physician assisted suicide for a loved one. Are their responses for themselves vs. for their loved ones similar or different?

2. Research what the laws are regarding physician assisted suicide in your state. If physician-assisted suicide is illegal,

a. has it nevertheless occurred and what happened?

b. have there been efforts to make it legal?

If PAS is legal in your state,

a. under what conditions?

b. how many PAS have occurred?

c. how many times have lawsuits been filed to try overturning laws in your state?

Research Navigator Guide: Social Gerontology

CHAPTER 14

The Resilience
of Elders of Color

Family Caregiving

Suggested Reading

Popular

1. Dilworth-Anderson, P., Gibson, B. W. Ethnic minority perspectives on dementia, family caregiving, and interventions. *Generations* Fall 1999, *23,* No. 23, p. 115 (*AN 2517930*).

The authors discuss the prevalence of dementia within ethnic minority groups in the U.S. Implications of the ethnic group's cultural values for developing formal services and interventions for people with dementia are also discussed. What impact might cultural values regarding family care and social conditions of specific ethnic minority groups have on their caregiving behavior?

2. "Ethnicity and dementia" is one of the topics listed on the website http://www.ethnicelderscare.net/. Three ethnic minority groups are identified: African American, Latino, and Asian American elders. Choose one of these three populations; discuss how dementia affects

this population and how families in that ethnic minority group are most likely to care for their affected elder.

3. Faculty members at Stanford Geriatric Education Center have produced teaching modules in ethnogeriatrics. Go to their website: http://www.stanford.edu/group/ethnoger/ and choose one population, i.e. Filipino, East Indian, African American. Go to the curriculum page. Discuss how they suggest teaching elder care vis-à-vis this particular ethnic minority group.

Scholarly

1. Hyunsook, Y., Hendricks, J. Asian ageing: context of change. *Ageing International* Spring 2003 *28,* No. 2 p. 115 (*AN 10289355*).

Asia is among the most rapidly aging regions in the world. Globalization has resulted in extensive changes in cultural values, especially among younger cohorts. Discuss the authors' description of communal accord and familial interdependence and how these have been affected by globalization in Asian countries.

2. Neufeld, A. et al Immigrant women: making connections to community resources for support in family caregiving. *Qualitative Health Research* Jul 2002, 12, No. 6, p. 751 (AN 6943280).

The authors report on an ethnographic study to understand how immigrant women caregivers accessed support from community resources. Discuss how the women did or did not overcome barriers to this support, including the importance of social networks.

3. Gudykunst, W. Lee, M., An agenda for studying ethnicity and family communication *Journal of Family Communication* 2001 1, No. 1, p. 75 (AN 4792967).

A theoretical model derived from cross-cultural research is described; this model can be applied to studying the ways ethnicity influences family communication. Explain why you agree or disagree with the authors' argument that the strength of cultural and ethnic identities are important factors that influence how family communication varies within and across ethnic groups.

Applied Research Exercises

1. Although much of the literature on elder care and caregiving focuses on ethnic and national *differences,* there are many similarities as well. After reviewing the articles above and the discussion of aging among

different ethnic minority groups in Chapter 14, and across countries in Chapter 2, make a list of cultural values regarding aging and elder care that are *similar* across two or more ethnic or national groups. Then make a list of cultural values that *differ* across these same groups. To what extent do these values result in similar or different activities among families in these ethnic or national groups?

2. Design an adult day health program that will serve older adults with dementia, providing them with social activities, meals, preventive health care, occupational therapy, and psychotherapy. This program should be designed to serve elders from multiple ethnic minority groups. What special features would you integrate into this program to serve the unique needs of these diverse elders, including staff training, languages, meals, and types of services provided?

Barriers to Care Faced by Ethnic Minority Elders

Suggested Reading

Popular

1. Taylor, L. Adult day-service providers fall victim to state budget deficit. *The Seattle Times* May 12, 2003.

The author states that adult day centers offer family caregivers much-needed breaks for round-the-clock caregiving. How does Washington state's $2.5 billion budget shortfall affect the state's momentum to work towards having their elders age in place?

2. King, W. Minority access to healthcare restricted—new county study focuses on disparities. *The Seattle Times* October 29, 1998.

Ethnic minority groups' limited access to health care is the focus of this article. According to the author, what factors affect access to health care? How do these barriers for ethnic minority populations affect care provided for elders from these disadvantaged groups?

3. Haas, JG. In search of a solution: care for the Hispanic elderly. *The Seattle Times* June 19, 2002.

The challenge of better serving older ethnic minorities is addressed in this article. The author points out that the AARP is making changes to reach out to Spanish-speaking populations. What are the specific measures that the AARP is taking to assist Latino elders? What do these measures tell us about barriers to health and social services for elders of color?

Research Navigator Guide: Social Gerontology

Scholarly

1. Rawl S., Champion V., Menon U., Foster J. The impact of age and race on mammography practices. *Health Care for Women International* Oct/Nov 2000, *21,* No. 7, p. 583 (*AN 3633915*).

This article discusses possible barriers to the use of mammography screening by various groups of women, and provides a measure of specific barriers. Data discussed in this article suggest that older African Americans and younger Caucasians had the highest total barrier scores, after controlling for education and income. What explains the high scores among these two groups? How can these results be used in developing interventions to improve rates of breast cancer screening among all groups?

2. Gaskin D., Hoffman C., Racial and ethnic differences in preventable hospitalizations across 10 states. *Medical Care Research & Review* Nov 2000 Supplement, *57,* No. 3, p. 85 (*AN 4585212*).

This study examined the relationship between race and ethnicity, and the likelihood of preventing hospitalization among African Americans and Latinos. The authors found that these groups were more likely than others to be hospitalized for health problems that could have been prevented. At the same time, the study found that older patients from both minority groups are less likely to receive preventive care than are white patients. According to the results of this study, what factors might explain discrepancy?

3. Eng, E., Earp, J., O'Malley, M., Altpeter, M., Rauscher, G., Mayne, L., Mahtews, H., Lynch, K., Qagish, B. Increasing use of mammography among older, rural African American women: results from a community trial. *American Journal of Public Health* Apr 2002, *92,* No. 4, p. 646 (*AN 6412725*).

The North Carolina Breast Cancer Screening Program aims to increase breast cancer screening among rural African American women over the age of 50. What did this research conclude in determining how to increase the use of screening mammography among low-income, ethnic minority women in rural settings?

Applied Research Exercises

1. Based on your understanding of the articles above and the discussion of the health status and access to health care among elders of color, make a list of barriers to access. Divide these by characteristics of the individual (e.g. age), cultural and societal or structural factors (e.g. reimbursement options). For each one of these barriers, describe briefly what actions could be taken to address these barriers and improve access for ethnic minority elders.

2. Imagine that you have been awarded a multi-million dollar contract to provide a cancer screening program for Latino and African American adults (ages 40+) in a large American city. Describe what you would do in the following areas to maximize the proportion of Latino and African American adults who participate in the screening program:
a. Outreach
b. Staffing (types of staff, ethnicity)
c. Cultural competence
d. Types of cancers to be screened

Outreach Programs to Ethnic Minority Elders

Suggested Reading

Popular

1. Yee, D., Tursi, C., Recognizing diversity and moving toward cultural competence: one organization's effort. *Generations* Fall 2003, *26,* No. 3, p. 54 (*AN8955324*).

The authors describe the efforts undertaken by a national association, the American Society on Aging (ASA), to respond to the demographic diversity among older adults in the U.S. and to prepare the work force that provides services and programs for them. Discuss the association's strategies to work towards its goals. To what extent have these objectives been met?

2. Center to offer comprehensive care for minority seniors. *Mental Health Weekly,* 7/21/2003, *13,* No. 27, p. 5 (*AN 10375316*).

The program described in this article targets older ethnic minorities in Los Angeles who have mental health needs, and aims to serve as a model of intervention for appropriate mental health services. What social aspects of mental health care for older people are targeted by this program? How does it go about training service providers to work with ethnic minority elders?

3. Swanbrow, D. Center sponsors research, outreach to help older minorities with health issues. *The University Record Online, University of Michigan.* November 11, 2002. http://www.umich.edu/~urecord/0102/Nov11_02/12.shtml

The National Institute on Aging has awarded a $3 million grant to the Michigan Center for Urban African American Aging Research, a unique collaboration between the University of Michigan and Wayne State University. Discuss how this funding will allow the center to sponsor outreach programs designed to promote the health of older African Americans and other minority populations in the greater Detroit area.

Scholarly

1. Levkoff, S., Sanchez, H. Lessons learned about minority recruitment and retention from the centers on minority aging and health promotion. *Gerontologist,* Feb 2003, *43,* No. 1, p. 18 (*AN 9158372*).

Suggestions are given regarding the recruitment and retention of ethnic minority elders as research participants, based on experiences in a program conducted to enhance research on minority health promotion. What factors lead to success in programs geared toward older ethnic minority individuals? What challenges must be expected in designing this kind of a program?

2. Coogle, C. The families who care project: meeting the educational needs of African American and rural family care givers dealing with dementia. *Educational Gerontology,* Jan 2002, *28,* No. 1, p. 59 (*AN 5655681*).

This article describes a program that addresses the needs of diverse rural and African American families who are coping with the challenges of caring for an elder with dementia. What educational needs does this program identify? What does the author suggest about cultural competence training for the provision of services to diverse caregiving families?

3. Wieck, KL. Health promotion for inner-city minority elders. *Journal of Community Health Nursing,* Fall 2000, *17,* No. 3, p. 131 (*AN 3506856*).

Project CAPABLE (Community Advocacy Promoting and Building Lifelines for Elders) provides health-promotion services to elders of color in inner city areas in Houston, Texas. List the factors mentioned in this article that can impede health promotion efforts for these populations. How does Project CAPABLE address these factors?

Applied Research Exercises

1. Based on your understanding of the articles above, as well as descriptions of ethnic minority elders' social and health status in Chapter 14, design a training program for nurses, social workers, and health educators, aimed at improving their cultural competence to work with at least *one* of the following groups of elders: African American, Latino, and American Indian. Your goal is to enhance the cultural awareness and communication skills of these professional groups, as well as their awareness of health problems and barriers to health care faced by these elders of color. What types of knowledge and skills would you

include in the training program? How would these differ from skills that professionals should have in working with the majority population or with elders from other ethnic groups?

2. Interview at least *three* health or social professionals who work directly with older adults (e.g. nurses, social workers, senior center directors). Ask each one to describe the diversity of the population that they serve, in terms of ethnicity, language, and gender. Have they learned or developed new skills by working with these different groups of elders? What are some of these skills that have been effective with specific groups?

Research Navigator Guide: Social Gerontology

CHAPTER 15

The Resilience of Older Women

Older Women's Economic Status

Suggested Reading

Popular

1. Associated Press. Social Security benefits keep many elderly women out of poverty. *The Seattle Times,* April 9, 1999.

According to this article, Social Security in the U.S. cuts in half the poverty gap between men and women, yet one in five older widows and one in four older divorced or single women are still poor. Describe ways in which the Social Security system helps improve older women's economic status, as well as some limitations in the system that prevent it from helping women in greatest need.

2. Kim, E. First lady exhorts women to save Social Security—Teleconference links cities across America. *The Seattle Times,* January 24, 1999.

The benefits of Social Security for older women are described in this article. What percentage of women would fall below the poverty level without Social Security? Why is it important for more women to become activists in determining the future of the Social Security system?

3. Cole, D. Looking at dollars and cents of widowhood. *The New York Times,* May 4, 2003.

This article discusses the need for women to account for possible widowhood when planning for their retirement. What specific financial suggestions does the article give for women as they face widowhood and possible remarriage in their later years?

Scholarly

1. Hungerford, T. The economic consequences of widowhood on elderly women in the United States and Germany. *Gerontologist,* Feb 2001, *41,* No. 1, p. 103 (*AN 4121235*).

The economic changes that older women face at widowhood in the United States and Germany are addressed in this report. How did the economic well-being of women in this study change following widowhood? What differences are discussed in retirement income systems in the United States and Germany that affect the economic well-being of older women in these two countries?

2. Mishra, G., Ball, K., Dobson, A., Byles, J., Warner-Smith, P. Which aspects of socioeconomic status are related to health in mid-aged and older women? *International Journal of Behavioral Medicine,* Sep 2002, *9,* No. 3, p. 263 (*AN 7386026*).

This study investigated the relationship between socioeconomic status and health outcomes in women aged 45 to 50 and women aged 70–75. What differences in socioeconomic status were found between women of the two age groups? What is the relationship observed in this study between socioeconomic status and health in older women?

3. Vartanian, T., McNamara, J. Older women in poverty: The impact of midlife factors. *Journal of Marriage & the Family,* May 2002, *64,* No. 2, p. 532 (*AN 6569767*).

Factors that contribute to older women's economic well-being were examined in this study. Compare midlife characteristics to late-life characteristics that may affect economic outcomes in old age. What evidence provided by the researchers supports these claims?

Applied Research Exercises

1. Interview at least 5 women in each of the following age groups: 20–30, 40–50, 65 and older. Your objective is to compare these groups regarding their financial planning for retirement and old age. Ask the following questions:

   a. How important is it for women to have a financial plan for their later years?

b. Have you developed a specific financial plan for yourself?

c. What sources of income do you expect to have (or in the case of women 65 and older, "what sources do you *currently* have") after age 65.

2. Many people are not aware of their potential earnings from Social Security until they approach their retirement. This is true even though the Social Security Administration has been sending individualized reports to working adults on their projected Social Security income if they retire at their age of eligibility for Social Security. Interview at least five working women in each of the following age groups: 30–40 and 50–60. Ask these women if they recall the latest report they have received from the SSA, and the approximate monthly Social Security income they can expect at retirement, based on that report. Are there differences between the two age groups in women's awareness and interest in their Social Security earnings? What other factors affect their recall and concern about this source of retirement income?

Resilience in Older Women

Suggested Reading

Popular

1. Briggs, D. Finding strength in difficult times. *The Seattle Times,* July 3, 1999.

This article examines resources such as religion that older women use in overcoming obstacles that may arise in their later years. According to this article, how is spirituality related to resilience in older women? To what extent do ethnic differences affect older women's sources of resilience?

2. Keene, L. Sweet little old ladies? Get real, says this group of free spirits—Crone celebrates former career women, activists, and feminists. *The Seattle Times,* July 5, 1999.

The strength and independence of older women is discussed in this article, highlighting groups such as "CRONE", which advocates the changing of stereotypes about older women. Give examples of ways in which women presented in this article are working to overcome these stereotypes.

3. Older women seek visibility—and more. *Christian Science Monitor,* October 11, 2000, *92,* Issue 224, p. 12 *(AN 3637779).*

The Older Women's League (OWL) is discussed in this article, which highlights the double standard between older men and women. Describe this

Research Navigator Guide: Social Gerontology

double standard and what is being done to overcome it. What other social conditions does OWL seek to change?

Scholarly

1. Bachay, J., Cingel, P. Restructuring resilience: Emerging voices. *Journal of Women & Social Work,* Summer 1999, *14,* No. 2, p. 162 (*AN 1827152*).

This study investigated resilience in minority women, focusing on three individual characteristics that enhanced their resilience. What were these three factors and how were they applied to minority women?

2. Felten, B., Resilience in a multicultural sample of community-dwelling women older than age 85. *Clinical Nursing Research,* May 2000, *9,* No. 2, p. 102 (*AN 3106561*).

The topic of this research is resilience in women over the age of 85 from diverse cultural backgrounds. How does this study define and set out to examine "resilience"? What differences were found in the resilience of these older women? What factors may account for these differences?

3. Humphreys, J. Resilience in sheltered battered women. *Issues in Mental Health Nursing,* Mar 2003, *24,* No. 2, p. 137 (*AN 9429171*).

In order to study resilience in battered women, the authors developed and tested a new measure, the Resilience Scale. Describe this scale. How does it define and measure this concept? Can the findings of this study be generalized to other groups of women?

Applied Research Exercises

1. Using the information gleaned from the readings above and from Chapter 15, define the concept of resilience in one paragraph. Make a list of biological, psychological, social, health, and cultural factors that can make a woman more or less resilient in old age. To what extent can any of these sources of resilience be learned or acquired by a younger woman as she prepares for successful aging?

2. Interview at least five women from diverse ethnic groups in each of the following age groups: 20–30, 40–50, 60 and older. Ask them to define "resilience" as they view this concept. Ask them to describe their sources of resilience and how these might help them if they face adversity in their own lives. Are there age differences in the definitions and sources of resilience described by these women? Are there any ethnic differences in their responses? To what extent have any of these women already tapped into their resilience at their current age, and how has this affected their confidence in coping with future challenges?

Health Problems Faced by Older Women

Suggested Reading

Popular

1. Duenwald, M. First year of hormone treatment is found to raise risk of heart attack. The *New York Times,* August 7, 2003.

This article reports that hormone replacement therapy almost doubles the risk of heart attack during the first year of treatment. Explain the effects of HRT on the body that increase the likelihood of heart attack. What do these findings suggest for the prescription of estrogen and progestin supplements?

2. Ostrom, C. Hormone replacement therapy: Is it worth the risks? *The Seattle Times,* July 14, 2002.

The author discusses the increased risk of having breast cancer, heart attacks, and strokes as a result of hormone replacement therapy (HRT). What are the benefits of HRT for post-menopausal women and what factors should women consider when deciding whether or not to take HRT?

3. Pollack, M. VITAL SIGNS: High Blood Pressure and Osteoporosis. *New York Times,* September 21, 1999.

A study of older women in Britain and the United States shows an association between high blood pressure and greater-than-normal loss of bone density. What accounts for this connection? What can older women do to protect against such aggravation of bone loss?

Scholarly

1. Kenney, J. Women's 'inner-balance': a comparison of stressors, personality traits and health problems by age groups. *Journal of Advanced Nursing,* Mar 2000, *31,* No. 3, p. 639 *(AN 6057654).*

This study examined differences in stressors and stress-related illnesses among women in different age groups. What stressors did all women have, regardless of age? What stressors were specific to older women? Did older women have more or less risk of stress-related illness than younger and middle aged women? What accounts for these differences?

2. Stegbauer, C., Sandstrom-Wakeling, S., Nied, L., Gambino, K., Zak, M., Duffy, E. The importance of mammography screening in elderly women. *Nurse Practitioner,* May 2003, *28,* No. 5, p. 50 *(AN 9667153).*

The significance of mammography screening in older women is discussed, as well as the symptoms of breast cancer in this population. The role of nurse practitioners in breast cancer prevention is also described. What is this role and how does it differ from the role of older women themselves in preventing breast cancer?

3. Delmas, P. D., Treatment of postmenopausal osteoporosis. *Lancet,* 6/8/2002, Vol. 359 Issue 9322, p. 2018 *(AN 6775225)*.

This article explores the option of using hormone replacement therapy in early postmenopausal women as a means of preventing osteoporosis. What factors influence the choice of treatment for reducing frequency of fractures? What non-pharmocological interventions does the author suggest for the prevention and treatment of osteoporosis?

Applied Research Exercises

1. Interview at least five women in each of the following age groups: 20–30, 40–50, and 60–70. Your objective is to determine how much they know about and are actively working to prevent osteoporosis. In each interview, ask the following questions:
   a. Have you ever had a Dexa-Scan or other test to measure bone mineral density?
   b. Do you know what osteoporosis is, and whether you are at risk for this condition?
   c. Do you have any close relatives who have been diagnosed for osteoporosis?
   d. What are you doing to prevent osteoporosis during and after menopause? (For women in their 20s, what are they currently doing to prevent this condition in the future? For women over 60, what are they doing to prevent and/or treat osteoporosis?
   As you examine the responses of each age group, consider whether age differences or experiences with menopause and/or osteoporosis have played a role in their answers.
2. Interview at least five women in each of the following age groups: 20 to 30; 40 to 50 and over age 60. The purpose of the interview is to find out how they have responded to the recent research results that hormone replacement therapy may actually increase the risk of heart attacks, stroke and breast cancer.
   a. Have you ever taken hormone replacement therapy (HRT) either to reduce menopausal symptoms or to strengthen your bone density? If so, for how long?
   b. Are you currently taking HRT?
   c. Do you feel you adequately understand the pros and cons of HRT?
   d. Did you change your health practices in terms of HRT based on recent research findings about the health risks associated with HRT? If you stopped taking HRT, how did your body react to this change? What other types of treatment have you used to deal with menopausal symptoms or to strengthen bone density?

Research Navigator Guide: Social Gerontology

CHAPTER 16

Social Policies
to Address
Social Problems

Older Americans Act (OAA)

Suggested Reading

Popular

  1. Adams, M. et al. Opportunities for older workers. *FDCH Congressional Testimony* September 3, 2003 (*AN 32Y3792899523*).

The author contends that skill training coupled with updated work experience is what older job seekers need in order to find employment. According to the authors, how has the "Earnings Gain" performance measure of the Workforce Investment Act (WIA) system discouraged older worker participation? Identify and discuss their recommendation regarding Title V of the Older Americans Act.

  2. When the Older Americans Act was reauthorized by Congress in 2002, the Family Caregiver Support Program was created. Discuss why this is an important program to those who care for older family members. http://www.aoa.dhhs.gov/wecare.

3. "Top 10 Senior Issues." *DollarSense* April 2001, p 2 (*AN 4428772*).

The article lists the top ten senior issues according to AARP. Besides the reauthorization of the Older Americans Act, what are other events that will impact the future of an aging population? Select three of the ten issues and discuss why they are concerns for seniors.

Scholarly

1. Clinton, W. J. Statement on signing the Older Americans Act amendments of 2000. *Weekly Compilation of Presidential Documents* November 20, 2000 *36,* No. 46, p. 2864 (*AN3862009*).

Read the former President's speech. Elaborate on why he thinks this legislation to revitalize the Older Americans Act is significant.

2. Nather, D. Senate clears reauthorization of 1965 Older Americans Act in states vs. nonprofits compromise. *CQ Weekly* October 28, 2000 *58* No. 42, 0. 2537.

The author reports on the provisions of the reauthorization of the OAA. Discuss the significance of the passage of this bill to the community service jobs program. According to the author, what programs were not included in the proposed reauthorization?

3. Mullins, B. A senior moment. *Congress Daily* November 3, 2000, p. 13 (*AN3741905*).

The Older American Caucus was established in 1995 after the disbanding of the Select Committee on Aging, as described in this article. Why did caucus members think approving the Older Americans Act was important? How did the caucus play a significant role in the reauthorization of the OAA and what are some of its current concerns?

Applied Research Exercises

1. The full text of the Older Americans Act can be found by logging on to http://www.aoa.dhhs.gov/Oaa/2000/hr782.html
The Older Americans Act (OAA) of 1965 is designed to provide assistance in the development of programs that will help people, 60 years and older, to maintain their independence and remain in their homes as long as possible.
Identify the variety of supportive services funded by the OAA, such as home-delivered meals, adult day care, health screenings, nutrition education and caregiver support. What are some gaps or limitations in the services offered? Discuss the eligibility age of 60 as a criterion for all beneficiaries, regardless of income. Do you see any problems with this universal age-based criterion? Recommend a program or service

Research Navigator Guide: Social Gerontology

not currently authorized by the OAA that you think would meet unaddressed needs of older adults.

2. One of the programs funded by the Administration on Aging is senior centers, which provide a range of social and health functions in communities throughout the United States. Many senior centers have seen declining membership in recent years; Explain this in terms of their older participants' dying. Critics maintain that senior centers are not doing enough in terms of outreach to the young-old and underserved populations such as ethnic minorities and gay and lesbian elders. Imagine that you were the director of a senior center that is at risk of losing its AoA funding because of declining participation.

   a. How would you go about determining the reasons for low participation rates?

   b. How would you identify underserved populations in your local community?

   c. What would you do in terms of outreach to such groups in your local community?

   d. What kinds of programs might you develop that better meet the needs of 1) the young-old, and 2) historically disadvantaged populations?

Entitlement Programs

Suggested Reading

Popular

1. Macguineas, M. The real state of the budget. *Atlantic Monthly,* Jan 2003, Vol. 291 Issue 1, p. 81, 1/2p, 2 charts, 3 graphs; (*AN 8879830*).

The U.S. federal budget for the year 2003 is discussed in terms of the allocation of funds for entitlement programs. How are funds allocated for entitlement programs, and how might this budget benefit the upper-middle class in the U.S.? Considering this effect, how will older individuals be affected by budgetary allocation for entitlement programs as discussed in this article?

2. Red George. *Economist,* July 5, 2003, *368,* No. 8331, p. 30 (*AN 10191763*).

The author criticizes Medicare reforms passed under President Bush, suggesting that the Republican Party is creating an entitlement program that will be harmful to the economy. According to this article, how is Medicare being used to create an economically harmful entitlement program? How do these budgetary changes affect segments of the older population in the United States?

Research Navigator Guide: Social Gerontology

3. Can't last. *Economist*, 1/10/2004, *370*, No. 8357, p. 23 (*AN 11908941*).

U.S. government spending and tax policy are discussed in this article. Due to an aging population and rising health care costs, entitlement programs are going to claim more of the economic output of the United States. What alternative ways of addressing this economic shift does the article present?

Scholarly

1. Gundersen, C., Ziliak, J. The role of food stamps in consumption stabilization. *Journal of Human Resources*, Sep 2003 Supplement, *38*, p. 1051 (*AN 11179981*).

The authors comment that the Food Stamp Program is the largest universal entitlement program in the social safety net, yet further research is needed to assess the impact of this program in household income and consumption. How does the Food Stamp Program affect older people? How did this program change throughout the 1980s and 1990s?

2. Medicaid proposal creating concerns among MH advocates. *Mental Health Weekly*, 3/10/2003, *13*, No. 10, p. 1 (*AN 9270893*).

The focus of this article is on the concern of mental health advocates about changes in Medicaid. Specifically, mental health advocates are concerned that this federal entitlement program will be abolished. What are the proposed changes discussed in the article? How would these changes affect mental health care for older adults?

3. Brown, DK. A context for teaching aging-related public policy. *Educational Gerontology*, Dec 99, *25*, No. 8, p. 711 (*AN 2705876*).

The author provides information about age-related public policy, discussing issues related to the cost and utilization of entitlement benefits for older people. What are the two conflicting schools of thought that can be used in teaching age-related public policy? Describe how they are different, and give reasons for ways in which each approach would be effective or ineffective.

Applied Research Exercises

1. After reading the articles above and reviewing the charts in Chapter 16 that illustrate the proportion of federal dollars allocated to entitlement programs, consider each of the following issues:
   a. List all the federal entitlement programs for which *only* older adults are eligible and the percentage of the federal budget allocated to these programs.
   b. List all the federal entitlement programs aimed at children and young adults, and the percentage of the federal budget allocated to these programs.

    c. With the U.S. experiencing its worst federal deficit ever, what changes should be made—if any—in eligibility for entitlement programs?

  2. Interview at least five men and women in each of the following age categories: 20–30, 40–50, 60 and older, regarding their attitudes toward age-entitlement and need-based entitlement programs. First define for them how these programs work, and give examples of each (e.g. Medicare is an age-based entitlement for Americans aged 65 and older; Medicaid is a program based on financial need). Ask each person you interview:

    a. What are the advantages and disadvantages of each type of entitlement program, to the recipient, to taxpayers, and to the government?

    b. How would they change these two types of entitlement programs so that they benefited people who are in greatest need?

    c. What changes would they make in the total federal budget in order to provide the "appropriate" levels of benefits in these entitlement programs, while at the same time providing adequate funding for military, national security, and other government services?

In analyzing the answers of your interviewees, consider how each respondent's age and gender has affected their responses, and their awareness of the debates surrounding entitlement programs.

Privatization of Social Security

Suggested Reading

Popular

  1. Hess, D. Social Security Privatization Bill Introduced, Action Unlikely *Congress Daily* January 21, 2003 (*AN 12088733*).

The author discusses how some lawmakers want a fixed percentage of Social Security tax contributions to be set aside for investment in private personal savings accounts. What is their reasoning behind this argument?

  2. Brock, F. Lost in the shuffle, a sign of strength for Social Security. *New York Times* April 13, 2003

The author reports that the trustees of social security extended two important deadlines. Identify these deadlines and why the trustees extended them. What proposals have the trustees made to subsidize the trust fund?

  3. Brock, F. Private accounts don't have to disturb Social Security. *New York Times* May 11, 2003

The author contends that the current administration and its opponents are in a struggle over whether to blend Social Security and the stock market.

The Shaw Plan may be a compromise. Describe this plan; are you in favor of it? Why or why not?

Scholarly

1. Francis, D. Playing politics over Social Security privatization. *Christian Science Monitor* June 17, 2002 94 No. 142, p. 17 (*AN 6824091*).

The author discusses how this debate over privatization is split down party lines. Identify the top three arguments on each side. Pick one argument on either side and discuss its validity.

2. House dems, women's groups pledge to block Social Security privatization. *Congress Daily* April 9, 2002, p. 9

The article reports that U.S. House democratic legislators and women's organizations oppose the privatization of social security. What are their reasons for opposing this direction? If the current system were displaced, what do they see as the potential hardships?

3. Norton, S. Shaw Blasts Gephardt, Democrats over social security. *Congress Daily* March 26, 2002, p. 4 (*AN 6417505*).

The author reports on the conflict between Republicans and Democrats over the issue of Social Security privatization. The central issue is the funding of private accounts as part of a Social Security reform plan. What are the arguments for and against the funding of private accounts? Summarize how each side sees its opposition using the upcoming election as a strategy.

Applied Research Exercises:

1. Interview at least five people across the age ranges 20–30, 40–50, 60 and older. Ask them what they see to be the advantages of the current Social Security system. Present them with a summary of one of the proposed models for privatization, as discussed in Chapter 16, and ask them what they see to be the advantages and disadvantages of such a model? Specifically ask them who they think would benefit the most from privatization, and who would be hurt the most. When you summarize their viewpoints on privatization, note any differences by age, gender or ethnic minority status.

2. Go to the websites of the following organizations:
   a. The Cato Institute
   b. The 20/30 Center
   c. National Committee to Preserve Social Security and Medicare, and
   d. The President's Commission to Study Social Security

   Review and summarize their arguments for and against privatization. In your summary, identify who would benefit the most from privatization, and who would benefit the least. Based on your review, would you support the privatization of Social Security or not? Provide reasons for the position that you hold.

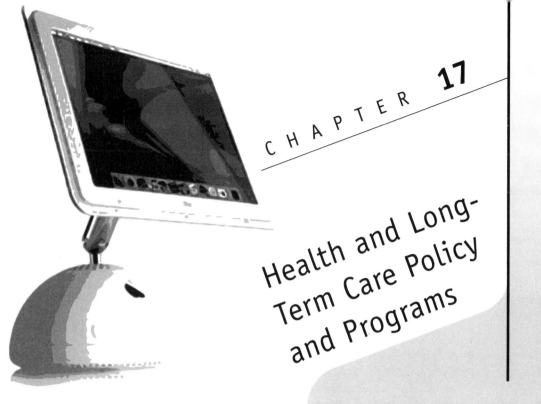

CHAPTER **17**

Health and Long-Term Care Policy and Programs

Innovations in Community-Based Long-Term Care

Suggested Reading

Popular

1. Is home care really working? *New York Times,* July 8, 2003.

This article presents the advantages and disadvantages of home care for older adults, explaining that while there may be budgetary advantages to home care, it is important to focus on the quality of care provided. What problems need to be addressed in order to provide effective home health care for frail elders?

2. Fremont Plans for Senior Services. *Public Management (U.S.),* March 2002, Vol 84 Issue 2 *(AN 6588473).*

The city of Fremont, California has created an action plan that addresses the needs of the community's senior citizens. Find three other cities that have implemented changes to make services more accessible to their older residents. Elaborate on these changes.

3. Perry, J. For most, there's no place like home. *U.S. News & World Report,* June 4, 2001, Vol 130 Issue 22 *(AN4487248).*

The author focuses on the effects of retirees on the communities where they relocate. Examples are provided of efforts by some cities to improve senior services. Select three cities where many seniors have retired and discuss how the communities have changed since a critical mass of older adults have settled there.

Scholarly

1. Bailey, L. Human services for the elderly and the role of university-community collaboration: Perceptions of human services agency workers. *Educational Gerontology,* Sept 2001, Vol. 27 Issue 6 *(AN 6263750).*

According to the U.S. Bureau of the Census, in 1998 the 65–74 age group (18.4 million) was eight times larger than in 1900; the 75–84 age group (12 million) was 16 times larger, and the 85 and older age group (4 million) was 33 times larger. It is anticipated that if this trend continues, by 2030 there will be about 70 million older Americans, more than twice their number in 1998. To meet the needs of the older population, governments, foundations, nonprofit organizations, and other groups will have to come up with ways to increase availability, accessibility, and adequacy of community-based services. The level and quality of community-based services are particularly important in supporting caregivers and recipients, and thus allowing older persons to remain in their own homes. Cite three studies that focus on how communities are working toward helping elders to remain in their homes.

2. Bodenheimer, T. Long-term care for frail elderly people—The On Lok Model. *New England Journal of Medicine,* 1999, *341,* No. 17, p. 1324 *(AN 2381003).*

This article gives information on long-term care for elderly people in the United States. The author discusses the On Lok Program in San Francisco, which serves as a model for other community-based long-term care programs. Discuss three aspects of this model that contribute to its success.

3. Cloutier-Fisher, D., Joseph, A. Long-term care restructuring in rural Ontario: Retrieving community service user and provider. *Social Science & Medicine,* 2000, *50,* No. 7/8, p. 1037 *(AN 2898865).*

The restructuring of community-based long-term care in Ontario, Canada is discussed in this article. What issues are addressed in this article regarding long-term care in rural communities?

Research Navigator Guide: Social Gerontology

Applied Research Exercises

1. In the October 2000 Special Issue of *The Gerontologist* (Vol 40 Issue 5 AN3724111), participants in a symposium on health promotion for older adults examined several community-based programs and discussed the problems of disseminating the findings of successful programs to other communities for their adoption. Design a system to streamline the process of diffusion and dissemination of information so that potential community organizations that could sponsor such programs can learn from each other's experiences.

2. Assume that cost is not a limiting factor and design an "ideal" community-based long-term care program for frail elders. Describe the elements of this program, staffing you would expect to hire, the types of elders to be served, and their maximum distance from the centralized service providers. What technology, if any, would you propose to expand the options and services for this community-based long-term care program?

The 2003 Medicare Prescription Drug Bill

Suggested Reading

Popular

1. Waller, D. Six questions about the new Medicare bill. *Time,* 12/8/2003, *162,* No. 23, p. 50 (*AN 11540307*).

This article explains the Medicare Prescription Drug legislation passed in November 2003, discussing changes in drug benefits and the introduction of private insurers into the Medicare plan. What major changes were made in these two areas? What concerns does the author express regarding costs and availability of prescription medications?

2. Lieberman, T. Privatizing Medicare. *Nation,* 7/7/2003, *277,* No. 1, p. 24 (*AN 10102069*).

The author critiques the new Medicare bills that were passed, commenting that these changes bring the social insurance program closer to privatization. Discuss the main points in her evaluation of recent reforms in Medicare. What does she say about the current trend in the way Health Maintenance Organizations serve beneficiaries?

3. Klein, J. Why the Democrats are all boxed in. *Time,* 12/1/2003, *162,* No. 22, p. 25 (*AN 11495987*).

Opposition to the 2003 Medicare Prescription Drug bill by the Democratic Party is discussed. According to the author, what is their stance on

Research Navigator Guide: Social Gerontology

the prescription-drug benefit in Medicare? Discuss the arguments presented in favor of and against the bill. How would these arguments affect services to older people?

Scholarly

1. Tieman, J., Taylor, M. House vs. Senate. *Modern Healthcare,* 10/20/2003, *33,* No. 42, p. 8 (*AN 11231796*).

The authors report on the debate regarding Medicare reform in 2003. What are some of the key points of debate between the U.S. House and Senate, according to this article? How do the issues raised affect health care for older adults in the United States?

2. Inglehart, JK. Prescription-drug coverage for Medicare beneficiaries. *New England Journal of Medicine,* 9/4/2003, *349,* No. 10, p. 923 (*AN 10712602*).

Details of the U.S. House and Senate versions of the Medicare prescription drug bill are discussed. What information does the author provide regarding the advantages to physicians of prescription drug coverage? According to the author, what were the main points of debate over this legislation between Democrats and Republicans?

3. Wechsler, J. Medicare reform offers pharmacy benefits, some competition. *Managed Healthcare Executive,* July 2003, *13,* No. 7, p. 12 (*AN 10300179*).

The author describes recent changes in Medicare prescription drug coverage, and issues related to the cost of providing quality care. According to the article, what are the advantages and disadvantages of providing prescription drug coverage under Medicare for retirees?

Applied Research Exercises

1. After reading the articles cited above, and the discussion in Chapter 17 of the Medicare Prescription Drug bill passed in 2003, make a chart that illustrates the following:
   a. Pre-2003 Medicare benefits, including provisions for prescription drugs
   b. Prescription drug and other benefits included in the reform bill passed in 2003
   c. Limitations on health services and prescription purchases placed by the new law
   d. The impact of each provision of the new law on specific segments of the older population (e.g. low and high income, elders, elders of color), on employers, and on providers such as physicians, hospitals, and drug companies

Research Navigator Guide: Social Gerontology

After reading the material cited above and constructing this chart, describe the overall strengths and weaknesses of the Medicare Prescription Drug Bill that became law in 2003.

2. Interview at least *10* men and women aged 45 to 65, to assess their knowledge about the 2003 Medicare Prescription Drug Bill, its provisions, and its potential impact on their health care when they become eligible for Medicare. Assuming the law is not modified by the time they qualify for Medicare, what are their thoughts on:

   a. How many medications do they currently use, and approximately how much do they spend per month on prescription drugs?

   b. What percentage of their prescription costs do they pay out-of-pocket versus percentage paid by their employer-provided insurance plan, a privately paid insurance plan, or through Medicaid?

   c. How do they think the new law will affect their prescription drug expenditures when they become eligible for Medicare, whether they continue to use the same medications they are currently using, or their health problems increase so that they will require more prescription drugs in old age?

   As you review the responses of your 10 interviewees, do you see differences by gender? By health and medication status? To what extent are their responses influenced by their level of knowledge about this new law?

Private Long-Term Care Insurance

Suggested Reading

Popular

1. House resolution promotes private long-term care insurance coverage for individuals. *Insurance Advocate* March 3, 2002 *112* No. 9, p. 34

This article reports on the United States Congress resolution that supports incentives for purchasing private long-term care insurance. The report states that Medicare and Medicaid do not cover the costs of long-term care. According to the article, how will the aging of baby boomers affect future long-term care costs?

2. Jones, C. What price LTCI? *Advisor Today,* Aug 2003, *98,* No. 8, p. 28 (*AN 10446633*).

The focus of this article is on current rates and premiums of long-term health insurance. What private health insurance carriers are represented by the Health Insurance Association of America, and what is the purpose of

Research Navigator Guide: Social Gerontology

this association? What are some models of long-term care insurance policies by these providers in covering options such as assisted living and home health care?

3. Expanding health insurance coverage. *Consumers' Research Magazine,* Jul 1999, *82,* No. 7, p. 41 *(AN 2105105).*

This report discusses an earlier proposal by the health insurance industry to offer tax incentives for people who purchase long term care insurance. What is the purpose of this proposal and what tax incentives would it provide for people who purchase private long term care insurance? What are the advantages and disadvantages of this proposal?

Scholarly

1. Government impedes LTC insurance, report says. *Nursing Homes Long Term Care Management* November 1999 *48* No. 11, p. 11.

An analysis is provided of a report that claims most Americans could buy private long-term care insurance. The author of the white paper maintains that publicly financed care has "anesthetized" Americans about the financial burden of long-term care so that they are unaware of the true costs. To what extent should federal and state government stop funding the cost of long-term care and require individuals to assume more responsibility for their own care?

2. Cohen, M., Miller, J., Weinrobe, M. Patterns of informal and formal caregiving among elders with private long-term care insurance. *Gerontologist,* Apr 2001, *41,* No. 2, p. 180 *(AN 4338733).*

The study described in this article examined options in caregiving among older people with private long-term care insurance. How does private long-term care insurance influence formal and informal care services for older adults? According to these authors, were claimants satisfied with their insurance policies? Why or why not?

3. Morris, G. LTCI carriers cool to bank channel. *Bank Investment Consultant,* Apr 2003, *11,* No. 4, p. 10 *(AN 9937994).*

A report on the recent annual conference of the Private Long-Term-Care Insurance Carriers is given, presenting challenges and advantages of private long term care insurance. What are the issues raised by that report? A grassroots bank distribution strategy is presented as an alternative to long-term care insurance. What does this involve?

Applied Research Exercises

1. Interview at least five people, both men and women, in the following age groups regarding long-term care insurance (LTCI): 20–30, 40–50, 60 and older. Ask them the following questions:

   a. What is long-term care insurance?

   b. Have they purchased a LTCI policy for themselves?

   c. Have their parents or other older relatives purchased LTCI?

   d. If the answer is "yes" to either or both questions b and c, what types of long-term care does this policy cover?

   e. If cost were not an issue, what is an ideal LTCI plan for themselves? In analyzing the responses to these questions, what differences do you observe by gender and age?

2. Based on your understanding of the articles above, and the description of long-term care insurance in Chapter 17, design a LTCI policy that would be most beneficial to the widest array of people if they needed long-term care after age 70. What types of services and LTC options would this policy cover? What would you recommend to make it affordable for most older adults? How would you vary the cost of this policy by the policy holder's age, gender, and family structure?

Research Navigator Guide: Social Gerontology